this book belongs to

Trudy Eckholdt

Joseph Smith,
the Man and the Seer

Joseph Smith, the Man and the Seer

by

Hyrum L. Andrus

Published by

DESERET BOOK COMPANY

Salt Lake City, Utah

1976

Lithographed by

in the United States of America

Affectionately Dedicated

to my parents,

MR. and MRS. N. LESLIE ANDRUS

of

Rexburg, Idaho

Acknowledgments

The writer is indebted to A. Hamer Reiser, President of the Sugar House Stake of Zion and Secretarial Assistant to the First Presidency, for suggesting and encouraging the publication of this volume. The suggestion was made after the writer had delivered an address on the Prophet Joseph Smith in the Sugar House Stake, December, 1959. President Reiser later read the manuscript of this book and offered helpful suggestions.

I am also indebted to certain of my colleagues at Brigham Young University for assistance given in the publication of this work. Dr. David H. Yarn, Jr., Dean of the College of Religious Instruction, read the manuscript and gave helpful suggestions. Professor Ralph A. Britsch offered helpful criticisms concerning grammar and organization. Dr. Truman Madsen, Chairman of the Department of Church History and Philosophy, assisted in locating some materials and made helpful suggestions. Others to whom credit is due include Professors Ivan J. Barrett and F. Kent Nielsen. Grateful acknowledgment is also made to the Brigham Young University Library and staff, and to the Church Historian's Office for important material that has gone into this volume. Finally, I am indebted to my wife, Helen Mae, for her support and encouragement over the years, as I have continued my research into the life and mission of Joseph Smith.

The Prophet Joseph Smith, an oil portrait by Alvin Gittins.

Preface

Few people, even among the Latter-day Saints, possess an adequate picture of Joseph Smith. This work is an effort to let those who knew the Prophet speak for themselves about his appearance, personal traits, and spiritual powers. The Mormon leader spoke modestly and with reserve about his spiritual experiences; and he was in no hurry to rush the account of such incidents into print. A revelation he received referred to the sacredness of spiritual things: "Remember that that which cometh from above is sacred, and must be spoken with care, and by constraint of Spirit."[1] Another revelation spoke of certain things revealed to the Prophet, and admonished, "Show them not unto any except them that believe."[2] For these and other reasons, Joseph Smith waited some time to commit to print many of the sacred events that ushered in the Dispensation of the Fulness of Times; and even then he reported but a few of the great manifestations that occurred.

This work is not an effort to reveal, in such a way as to exploit the phenomenal, certain things that Joseph Smith but modestly alluded to in his history. It is the writer's hope that as this publication will make more available many little-known incidents that reveal the Prophet's character and spiritual powers, these incidents will present a more accurate picture of the Mormon leader and point out more clearly the source of his ideas. The evidence presented in this volume indicates the fallacy of certain theories that Joseph Smith was a dreamer, an epileptic, a spiritualist, a mystic, or a deceiver. Many of the Prophet's associates participated, directly and indirectly, in the revelations,

---

[1]Doctrine and Covenants 63:64.
[2]Moses 1:42.

visions, and other spiritual manifestations that he received. They were men of sound minds and of good character. Their testimonies corroborate those of Joseph Smith and prove that the great manifestations he received were not mystical nor deceptive in nature. They, too, saw and bore witness.

Nowhere else in the annals of history can such evidence be found to support the reality of revelation from God—from a source of enlightened truth that is consistent within itself, uplifting in its power and influence, and demonstrable in the lives of others. When the time comes that skeptics learn of the power of faith and when those who scoff at spiritual truth come to understanding, Joseph Smith will be studied more thoughtfully and considerately by conscientious students.

CONTENTS

L. A. Ramsay portrait of the Prophet Joseph Smith. Completed in 1910, the canvas hangs in the Salt Lake Temple.

I.

Joseph Smith the Man

"I feel like shouting hallelujah, all the time, when I think that I ever knew Joseph Smith, the Prophet," declared Brigham Young.[1] Other associates of the Mormon Prophet were equally enthusiastic in their praise of him. Such a remarkable character comes rarely on the scene of history; and, after making his appearance, seldom does he leave such an indelible imprint upon the lives of others as did the Prophet Joseph Smith.

The man Joseph was a commanding figure with a magnetic personality. He possessed a "distinguishing mark," a "noble grandeur," that set him apart from other men.[2] A United States Artillery Officer wrote in 1842: "Joseph . . . is a noble looking fellow, a Mahomet every inch of him. Who will say that the Mormon Prophet is not among the great spirits of the age?"[3]

Josiah Quincy, Jr., son of the president of Harvard and himself later mayor of Boston, visited Nauvoo with his friend, the Hon. Charles Francis Adams, in May, 1844. Neither was a friend of Joseph Smith nor of the cause he espoused. In his diary, Adams referred to Mormonism as a "delusion" and to the Prophet as "its mountebank apostle."[4] Quincy spoke of the "monstrous claims" of Mor-

---

[1]*Journal of Discourses*, III. 51. Hereafter abbreviated *J. D.*, followed by appropriate volume and page number.
[2]Statement by Lydia Bailey, later the wife of Newel Knight. *Journal History*, October 29, 1833.
[3]Reprinted in *Millennial Star*, III (September, 1842), p. 84.
[4]Henry Adams, *Charles Francis Adams Visits the Mormons in 1844*, (Boston, 1952), pp. 20-23. From the *Proceedings of the Massachusetts Historical Society*, LXVIII, 1944-1947.

monism and termed the Prophet's discussion of the restored
gospel as "wild talk" wherein he "supported his views by
the glib recitation of a number of texts." But despite his
sarcasm Quincy confessed that he stood "helpless before
the puzzle." One thing he could understand—that somehow this "man of commanding appearance" had touched
the lives of thousands and was indeed a force to be reck-
oned with in the earth. Quincy's respect for this obvious
fact caused him to open his account of his visit to Nauvoo
with the following words:

> It is by no means improbable that some future
> text-book, for the use of generations yet unborn,
> will contain a question something like this: What
> historical American of the nineteenth century has
> exerted the most powerful influence upon the des-
> tinies of his countrymen? And it is by no means
> impossible that the answer to that interrogatory
> may be thus written: Joseph Smith, the Mormon
> Prophet. And the reply, absurd as it doubtless
> seems to most men now living, may be an obvious
> commonplace to their descendants. . . . The man
> who established a religion in this age of free
> debate, who was and is to-day accepted by hun-
> dreds of thousands as a direct emissary from the
> Most High,—such a rare human being is not to
> be disposed of by pelting his memory with
> unsavory epithets.[5]

Less than a year earlier, a non-Mormon editor spoke
of Joseph Smith as "one of the most remarkable men of
the present, or in fact of any other age." While asserting
that he was in no way a believer "in Mormonism, or in our
friend Joseph the Prophet, as a *divine Teacher*," the editor
compared him with Mahomet, and the revolution the
Prophet was effecting with that which Mahomet had ini-

---

[5]Josiah Quincy, *Figures of the Past* (Boston, 1883), pp. 376-400.

tiated centuries before. But Mahomet "appeared at an age when darkness, idolatry and superstition cast upon the world the shadows of mental stupor and moral death," he observed.

How different stands the case with Joseph Smith, the Prophet, and Apostle of Mormon. He appears in the middle of the nineteenth century. The full glory of brightness and revelation is in the very zenith of the Christian firmament, and in a country too, most distinguished for enlighten- ment, and the least prejudiced of bigotry and fanaticism, ancient manners, and inherited forms of religion. Still his success is no less remarkable, although in an age so much less susceptible to the wicked designs of Priestcraft, and the designing schemes of ambitious men.[6]

Those who knew Joseph Smith personally were par- ticularly impressed by his greatness. James Leech and Bathsheba W. Smith spoke of him as being "different from any other man" they had ever seen.[7] To the latter, he was "an extraordinary man," who "looked the soul and honor of integrity."[8] Joseph Taylor, Sr., expressed the belief that the Prophet was "one of God's noblemen,"[9] while Wiley Payne Allred wrote that he was "the most noble man" he had ever seen.[10] Jesse N. Smith declared the Mormon leader to be "incomparably the most God-like man I ever saw."[11] And John M. Chidester reported that, as he met the Prophet and shook hands with him, he was im- pressed that he "stood face to face with the greatest man

[6]*Lee County Democrat*, Fort Madison, III (July 29, 1843), p. 2.
[7]*Juvenile Instructor*, XXVII, pp. 152, 344.
[8]*Ibid.*, p. 344.
[9]*Ibid.*, p. 202.
[10]*Ibid.*, p. 256.
[11]*Ibid.*, p. 23.

on earth."[12] Amasa M. Lyman gave a more detailed account of meeting Joseph Smith:

> When he grasped my hand in that cordial way (known to those who have met him in the honest simplicity of truth), I felt as one of old in the presence of the Lord, my strength seemed to be gone, so that it required an effort on my part to stand on my feet; but in all this there was no fear, but the serenity and peace of heaven pervaded my soul, and the still small voice of the spirit whispered its living testimony in the depths of my soul, where it has ever remained, that he was a Man of God.[13]

Such sentiments were widespread and of lasting significance among the Prophet's acquaintances. As James B. Bracken recalled Joseph's conduct during a trying experience in Missouri, he observed, "I never saw a nobler looking or acting man than Joseph Smith appeared on that occasion."[14] Said Daniel D. McArthur, "To me he seemed to possess more power and force of character than any ordinary man. I would look upon him when he was with hundreds of other men, then, he would appear greater than ever."[15]

According to Angus M. Cannon:

> He was one of the grandest samples of manhood that I ever saw walk or ride at the head of a legion of men. In listening to him as he has addressed the Saints his words have so affected me that I would rise upon my feet in the agitation that would take hold of my mind.[16]

---

[12]*Ibid.*, p. 151.
[13]*Deseret News*, VIII, p. 117.
[14]*Juvenile Instructor*, XXVII, p. 203.
[15]*Ibid.*, pp. 128-129.
[16]*Young Woman's Journal*, XVII, p. 546.

Of the Prophet's appearance as a Lieutenant General at the head of the Nauvoo Legion, Lyman L. Woods recalled, "I have seen him on a white horse wearing the uniform of a general. . . . He was leading a parade of the Legion and looked like a god."[17] Mary Ann Winters also related:

> I saw him on parade at the head of the Nauvoo Legion, looking noble and grand as a leader could do. His commanding presence could be discerned above all others, and all eyes were centered on him, as he rode back and forth giving the commands of his office.[18]

Even those previously prejudiced against the Prophet because of the tide of hatred and persecution that was raised against him were impressed when they had the opportunity personally to meet and speak with him. Many of the officials who would have taken his life, during the Missouri difficulties, "turned in his favor on forming his acquaintance."[19] While a prisoner in Missouri, Joseph Smith was delivered into the custody of his bitter enemy, General Moses Wilson. Later General Wilson said of him, "He was a very remarkable man. I carried him into my house, a prisoner in chains, and in less than two hours my wife loved him better than she did me." Some years later, when the Wilsons had moved to Texas, the General was engaged in raising a mob against some Mormon elders in that area. Upon hearing of these plans, Mrs. Wilson, although an

---

[17]Cited in Nels Anderson, *Desert Saints* (Chicago, 1942), p. 5. A reporter recorded the sentiments of Lucy Diantha Morley Allen, aged ninety, when asked to express her memories of Joseph Smith:
    Tears came to Sister Allen's eyes when she recalls his looks, while speaking to the Saints, and also how majestic he looked when he rode on his great black horse at the head of the Nauvoo Legion.
    She says the only words that express his looks and actions are: "Surely he was a man of God."—*Young Woman's Journal*, XVIII, p. 538.
    [18]*Ibid.*, XVI, p. 558.
    [19]Reported by Daniel Tyler, *Juvenile Instructor*, XXVII, p. 491.

aged lady, mounted her horse and rode thirty miles to warn the elders. No doubt her esteem for the Prophet largely motivated her in this action.[20]

Shortly after the family of Joseph Smith, Sr., moved to Far West, Missouri, in the summer of 1838, difficulties arose between the Saints and the mob element in that area. It started at an election held at Gallatin, the county seat of Daviess County, Missouri, when a group of non-Mormons attempted to prevent certain of the brethren from voting. The Prophet was not present at the time. A struggle occurred in which several non-Mormons were hurt, and the report was afterward circulated that Joseph Smith had himself killed seven men and intended to organize the Saints and exterminate all who were not of the Mormon faith.

A few days thereafter, Joseph was at the home of his parents, writing a letter, when a large body of armed men came to the door. Eight of their officers dismounted and entered the house, stating that they had come "to kill Joe Smith and all the 'Mormons.'" When Mother Smith informed them that her son had not been in Daviess County, one of the officers rejoined, "There is no doubt that the report is perfectly correct; it came straight to us, and I believe it; and we were sent to kill the Prophet and all who believe in him, and I'll be d——d if I don't execute my orders." After some further comments, Joseph arose from his writing table and was introduced by his mother. As they stared at him, "he smiled, and stepping towards them, gave each of them his hand, in a manner which convinced them that he was neither a guilty criminal nor yet a hypocrite." He then sat down and explained to them the attitude of the Saints and what their course had been amid the difficulties that had been heaped upon them. After

[20]J. D., XVII, p. 92.

talking to them for some time, he turned and said, "Mother, I believe I will go home now—Emma will be expecting me." At this, two of the officers sprang to their feet and suggested that he should not go alone and that they would attend him in order to protect him. As the three men left the house, Mother Smith overheard the following conversation among the officers who remained at the door:

1st Officer. "Did you not feel strangely when Smith took you by the hand? I never felt so in my life."

2nd Officer. "I could not move. I would not harm a hair of that man's head for the whole world."

3rd Officer. "This is the last time you will catch me coming to kill Joe Smith, or the 'Mormons' either."

1st Officer. "I guess this is about my last expedition against this place. I never saw a more harmless, innocent-appearing man than the 'Mormon' Prophet."

2nd Officer. "That story about his killing those men is all a d——d lie—there is no doubt of it; and we have had all this trouble for nothing; but they will never fool me in this way again; I'll warrant them."[21]

Because of the Prophet's striking figure and personality, many people immediately recognized him upon seeing him, without an introduction. Andrew Workman and Jane Snyder Richards later wrote that they "recognized him at first sight."[22] As a young man, George Q. Cannon

[21]Lucy Mack Smith, *History of Joseph Smith* (Salt Lake City, 1954), pp. 254-256.

[22]*Juvenile Instructor,* XXVII, p. 641; *Young Woman's Journal,* XVI, p. 550. In 1841, Maria J. Woodard, then a girl of seventeen, walked with Alfonzo L. Young, her guardian, and others from Middle Tennessee to Nauvoo. She later stated that she and Young "both knew the Prophet" as soon as they saw him.— *Ibid.,* XVII, p. 543.

was with a group of immigrants who traveled up the Mis-
sissippi River by boat to Nauvoo. As a large concourse of
people gathered to meet them, young Cannon identified the
Prophet immediately. "He would have known him among
ten thousand," Cannon later wrote in his biography of the
Mormon leader. "There was that about him which to the
author's eyes, distinguished him from all the men he had
ever seen."[23]   Mary Alice Lambert also said:

> I knew him the instant my eyes rested upon
> him, and at that moment I received my testimony
> that he was a Prophet of God, for I never had
> such a feeling for mortal man as thrilled my being
> when my eyes first rested upon Joseph Smith. He
> was not pointed out to me. I knew him from all
> the other men, and, child that I was (I was only
> fourteen) I knew that I saw a Prophet of God.[24]

Emmeline B. Wells, who became a noted figure among
Mormon women, gave a similar testimony. Though she
"had not formed any idea" of the Prophet's appearance
before meeting him, she wrote:

> At last the boat reached the upper landing,
> and a crowd of people were coming toward the
> bank of the river. As we stepped ashore the
> crowd advanced, and I could see one person who
> towered away and above all the others around
> him; in fact I did not see distinctly any others. His
> majestic bearing, so entirely different from anyone
> I had ever seen (and I had seen many superior
> men) was more than a surprise. It was as if I
> beheld a vision; I seemed to be lifted off my feet,
> to be as it were walking in the air, and paying no
> heed whatever to those around me. I made my
> way through the crowd, then I saw this man whom

[23]George Q. Cannon, The Life of Joseph Smith, (Salt Lake City, 1888),
p. xxvii.
[24]Young Woman's Journal, XVI, p. 554.

I had noticed, because of his lofty appearance, shaking hands with all the people, men, women, and children. Before I was aware of it he came to me, and when he took my hand, I was simply electrified—thrilled through and through to the tips of my fingers, and every part of my body, as if some magic elixir had given me new life and vitality. I am sure that for a few minutes I was not conscious of motion. I think I stood still, I did not want to speak, or be spoken to. I was over-whelmed with indefinable emotion. . . .

I was in reality too full for utterance. I think had I been formally presented to the Prophet, I should have fallen down at his feet, I was in such a state of ecstasy. The one thought that filled my soul was, I have seen the Prophet of God, he has taken me by the hand, and this testimony has never left me in all the "perils by the way." It is as vivid today as ever it was. For many years, I felt it too sacred an experience even to mention.[25]

George Miller, later a prominent bishop in the Church, also recognized the Prophet upon sight, without an intro-duction. Miller had befriended some of the Saints when they were driven from Missouri. As a prominent farmer in Illinois, he fed some and gave work to others. Among the latter were Samuel and Don Carlos Smith, the Prophet's brothers, from whom Miller later learned that the Prophet had made his escape from Missouri. Shortly thereafter the future bishop, who had not yet heard a sermon by a Latter-day Saint elder, met the Mormon leader. The successful farmer spoke of his feelings upon meeting the penniless Prophet, in the following words:

As I was in the habit of riding out every fair day, on a bland, bright morning I prevailed on my wife to indulge in the luxury of a ride on horseback

---

[25]*Young Woman's Journal,* XVI, p. 555.

to visit our tenants on the farm. On our return home, as we were leisurely riding along, I perceived a carriage containing a number of persons meeting us, and as we neared it, the appearance of a large man, sitting in front driving, seemed familiar to me, as if I had always known him, and suddenly the thought burst into my mind that it was none other than the Prophet Joseph Smith. Indeed my whole frame was in a tremor at the thought, and my heart seemed as if it were coming up into my mouth. Getting in speaking distance, he suddenly reined up his horses, as if making ready to speak. I was much agitated as the words came from his mouth. "Sir, can you tell me the way to the farm of a Mr. Miller, living somewhere in the direction I am going?" Instead of answering him directly, my reply was, "I presume, sir, that you are Joseph Smith, Jr., the Mormon Prophet." "I am, sir," he replied, adding, "I also presume that you are the Mr. Miller whose farm I inquired for." "I am, sir." He then introduced me to his wife and family, and thus a formal (or rather informal) introduction passed between us and our families.[26]

Many people spoke of Joseph Smith as being strikingly handsome. Josiah Quincy observed, "A *fine-looking man* is what the passer-by would instinctively have murmured upon meeting the remarkable individual who had fashioned the mould which was to shape the feelings of so many thousands of his fellow mortals."[27] A visitor at Nauvoo agreed;[28] and from Washington a member of Congress wrote to his wife, after seeing the Prophet, "He is . . . what you ladies would call a very good-looking man."[29]

Lydia Bailey described Joseph Smith as possessing

---

[26]*A Mormon Bishop and His Son,* ed., H. M. Mills (London, nd.), pp. 32-33.
[27]Quincy, *op. cit.,* p. 381.
[28]*History of the Church,* IV, p. 566.
[29]*The Historical Record,* VII (January, 1888), p. 476.

"a tall, well-built form, with the carriage of an Apollo, brown hair, handsome blue eyes, which seemed to dive down to the innermost thoughts with their sharp, penetrating gaze, a striking countenance, and with manners at once majestic yet gentile, dignified yet exceedingly pleasant."[30] Wandle Mace gave a similar description:

> He was a fine-looking man, tall and well-proportioned, strong and active, light complexion, blue eyes, and light hair, and very little beard. He had a free and easy manner, not the least affectation yet bold and independent, and very interesting and eloquent in speech.[31]

Others gave more detailed descriptions of Joseph Smith. A correspondent of the *New York Herald*, after visiting Nauvoo in 1842, spoke of him as "one of the most accomplished and powerful chiefs of the age." He then gave what Helen Mar Whitney, an intimate friend of the Prophet, termed a "truthful description"[32] of the Mormon leader, in the following words:

> Joseph Smith, the president of the church, prophet, seer, and revelator, is thirty-six years of age, six feet high in pumps, weighing two hundred and twelve pounds. He is a man of the highest order of talent and great independence of character—firm in his integrity—and devoted to his religion; . . . as a public speaker he is bold, powerful, and convincing; . . . as a leader, wise and prudent, yet fearless as a military commander; brave and

---

[30]*Journal History*, October 29, 1833. See *Young Woman's Journal*, XVII, p. 544, for a statement by Elias Cox.

[31]"Journal of Wandle Mace, 1809-1890," Typewritten copy, Brigham Young University Library, p. 38. Bathsheba W. Smith wrote:
The Prophet was a handsome man,—splendid looking, a large man, tall and fair and his hair was light. He had a very nice complexion, his eyes were blue, and his hair a golden brown and pretty—*Young Woman's Journal*, XVI, p. 549.

[32]Helen Mar Whitney, "Scenes and Incidents in Nauvoo," *Woman's Exponent*, X (December 1, 1881), pp. 97-98.

determined as a citizen, worthy, affable, and kind;
bland in his manners, and of noble bearing.[33]

The *Weekly Gazette,* of St. Louis, Missouri, published a rather detailed description of Joseph Smith, in May,
1844. His chest and shoulders were said to be "broad
and muscular," while his hands were "small for his propor-
tions." His feet, however, were large. Continued the
Gazette:

> The shape of his head is a very oblong oval,
> the coronal region high, denoting a resolved will,
> the basal and occipital full, indicating powerful
> impulses, and the frontal retreating, although the
> region devoted by phrenologists to the organiza-
> tion of the perceptive powers is unusually promi-
> nent. His forehead is white, without a furrow,
> and notwithstanding the small facial angle, some-
> what symmetrical. His hair is quite light and fine,
> complexion pale, cheeks full, temperament evi-
> dently sanguine, lips thin, rather than thick.
>
> But the Prophet's most remarkable feature
> is his eye. Not that it is very large, or very bright,
> very thoughtful or very restless, or even very deep
> in its expression or location; for it is usually neither
> of them. The hue is light hazel, and it is shaded,
> and, at times, almost veiled by the longest, thickest
> light lashes you ever saw belonging to a man. The
> brows are also light and thick indeed, precisely
> of that description called beetle-brow.
>
> His voice is low and soft, and his smile, which
> is frequent, is agreeable.
>
> The Prophet's wife is reported to have said
> of him, "No painting of him could catch his ex-
> pression, for his countenance was always chang-
> ing to match his thoughts and feelings."[34]

---

[33]*New York Herald,* February 19, 1842. Reprinted in *Millennial Star,* III
(May, 1842), p. 8.

[34]Cited in Edwin F. Parry, *Stories about Joseph Smith the Prophet* (Salt Lake
City, 1934), pp. 158-160.

Parley P. Pratt left perhaps the best picture of the Prophet's person and character. This description from his gifted pen was written shortly after the martyrdom:

President Joseph Smith was in person tall and well built, strong and active; of light complex-ion, light hair, blue eyes, very little beard, and of an expression peculiar to himself, on which the eye naturally rested with interest, and was never weary of beholding. His countenance was ever mild, affable, beaming with intelligence and benev-olence; mingled with a look of interest and an un-conscious smile, or cheerfulness, and entirely free from all restraint or affectation of gravity; and there was something connected with the serene and steady penetrating glance of his eye, as if he would penetrate the deepest abyss of the human heart, gaze into eternity, penetrate the heaven and comprehend all worlds.

He possessed a noble boldness and independ-ence of character; his manner was easy and famil-iar; his rebuke terrible as the lion; his benevolence unbounded as the ocean; his intelligence universal, and his language abounding in original eloquence peculiar to himself—not polished—not studied—not smoothed and softened by education and re-fined by art; but flowing forth in its own native simplicity, and profusely abounding in variety of subject and manner. He interested and edified, while, at the same time, he amused and entertained his audience; and none listened to him who were ever weary with his discourse. I have even known him to retain a congregation of willing and anxious listeners for many hours together, in the midst of cold or sunshine, rain or wind, while they were laughing at one moment and weeping the next. Even his most bitter enemies were generally over-come, if he could once get their ears. . . .

In short, in him the character of a Daniel and

a Cyrus were wonderfully blended. The gifts, wisdom and devotion of a Daniel were united with the boldness, courage, temperance, perseverance and generosity of a Cyrus. And had he been spared a martyr's fate till mature manhood and age, he was certainly endowed with powers and ability to have revolutionized the world in many respects, and to have transmitted to posterity a name associated with more brilliant and glorious acts than has yet fallen to the lot of mortal.[35]

Physically, the Prophet was a powerful man. "He was as quick as a squirrel and as strong as a mountain lion," said Lyman L. Woods, "but he was as gentle as a lamb."[36] Said another, "He was about six feet tall, sound bodied, very strong and quick—no breakage about his body."[37]

On the frontier, where Joseph spent much of his life, the measure of a man was largely determined by his strength and agility. Wrestling was a common sport, and on many occasions the Prophet engaged in it either for sport or to meet the challenges forced upon him. While visiting Ramus, Illinois, he wrote in his *Journal*, "I wrestled with William Wall, the most expert wrestler in Ramus, and threw him."[38] Another such instance was related by Major Joseph McGee of Gallatin, Missouri, who said, "I saw Joseph Smith throw John Brassfield, the champion wrestler of the country, the first two falls out of a match of three. He was a powerful man."[39] Those who knew the Prophet gave similar reports. Said Enoch E. Dodge, "I have seen him run, jump, wrestle and pull sticks many times, and he was always winner."[40] Again from another, "I've seen the

[35]*The Historical Record*, op. cit., pp. 575-576.
[36]Cited in Anderson, op. cit., p. 5.
[37]Statement by Elam Cheney, Sr., *Young Woman's Journal*, XVII, pp. 539-540.
[38]*History of the Church*, V, p. 302.
[39]"Special Correspondence from Caldwell County, Missouri," *Deseret Evening News*, September 10, 1904, p. 23.

Prophet wrestle, and run, and jump, but have never seen him beaten. In all that he did he was manly and almost godlike."[41]

While the Prophet and others were imprisoned in Missouri, they were sent to Daviess County under guard and turned over to a group of the strongest and roughest men in that county. The reputed champion wrestler of Daviess County challenged the Prophet to a wrestling match, which Joseph at first declined to engage in because he was a prisoner and felt that he could not participate in such activities under the circumstances. But, after being encouraged by the guards and after the man had promised not to get angry if he should be thrown, the Prophet consented. The Daviess County wrestler sought to use all the trickery known to him in his effort to throw the Prophet, but he failed. Finally, Joseph made his first real attempt and threw his antagonist flat on his back in a puddle of water. This made the Missourian angry, even though he had agreed to restrain himself, but his associates interfered and thereafter subjected him to much ridicule over the matter.[42]

Pulling sticks was another sport in which the Prophet often engaged. The contestants would sit upon the floor facing each other, with a sturdy stick between them, and then see which one could pull the other up from his seated position. But in such tests of strength, said Benjamin F. Johnson, "he never found his match."[43] Joseph recorded one such example in his *Journal,* "In the evening, when pulling sticks, I pulled up Justice A. Morse, the strongest man in Ramus, with one hand."[44] On another occasion,

[40]*Young Woman's Journal,* XVII, p. 544.
[41]*Ibid.,* pp. 537-538.
[42]See *Autobiography of Andrew Jenson,* pp. 164-165.
[43]Benjamin F. Johnson, "An Interesting Letter," unpublished letter from Johnson to George S. Gibbs, April to July 1903, Brigham Young University Library, p. 4.
[44]*History of the Church,* V, p. 302.

the Prophet was traveling away from Nauvoo when an attempt was made to kidnap him and to carry him to Missouri, to be turned over to his former persecutors. But the Prophet's enemies were frustrated when certain brethren intercepted the kidnapping party and issued legal procedures against them, whereupon the two hostile bands found it necessary to travel together to Nauvoo. Upon his return the Prophet spoke to the Saints, declaring:

> I am well—I am hearty. . . . I feel as strong as a giant. I pulled sticks with the men coming along, and I pulled up with one hand the strongest man that could be found. Then two men tried, but they could not pull me up.[45]

The Prophet often applied his physical exercises and sports toward the accomplishment of wholesome purposes. While studying Greek and Latin, he would interrupt his work to play with the children in their games and to give himself exercise, and when sufficiently relaxed he would return to his studies.[46] While preaching one day,

> He said it tried some of the pious folks to see him play ball with the boys. He then related a story of a certain prophet who was sitting under the shade of a tree amusing himself in some way, when a hunter came along with his bow and arrow, and reproved him. The prophet asked him if he kept his bow strung up all the time. The hunter answered that he did not. The prophet asked why, and he said it would lose its elasticity if he did. The prophet said it was just so with his mind, he did not want it strung up all the time.[47]

The development of friendship and sociability was another worthy goal sought by the Prophet through the

---

[45]*Ibid.,* p. 466.
[46]*Juvenile Instructor,* XXVII, p. 302.
[47]*Ibid.,* p. 472.

use of sports. When his brother Hyrum reproved him for playing a game of ball with some young men in Nauvoo, stating that such conduct was not becoming to a Prophet of the Lord, Joseph replied, "Brother Hyrum, my mingling with the boys in a harmless sport like this does not injure me in any way, but on the other hand it makes them happy and draws their hearts nearer to mine; and who knows but there may be young men among them who may sometime lay down their lives for me!"[48]

Strength of body was combined in the Prophet with an indomitable will and a supreme courage in doing right. He and his brother Hyrum were said to be "as brave as lions."[49] A non-Mormon reporter stated that the Mormon leader possessed that degree of "concentrated moral and spiritual energy [that] fears no combat, and although we cannot say it exactly courts danger, it never flies from the post of duty on its approach."[50] In a letter to James Arlington Bennett, Joseph himself wrote, "I never knew what it was, as yet, to fear the face of clay, or the influence of man."[51]

The Prophet's reputation was founded in deeds of courage. It is common knowledge that as a boy he had typhus fever, which caused among its aftereffects, a severe pain in his shoulder that subsequently "shot like lightning" down his side into the bone of his leg. After efforts to relieve the pain by making incisions in his leg had failed, his doctors decided to amputate it at the knee. But his mother prevailed upon them to try once more to save the leg, and it was decided to cut away the infected parts of the bone. Since anaesthetics were not known in those

---

[48]Related by Lorenzo Snow. Cited in *Stories about Joseph Smith the Prophet,* p. 97.
[49]*Millennial Star,* III (September, 1842), p. 84.
[50]Reprinted in *ibid.,* (August, 1842), pp. 65-66.
[51]*History of the Church,* V, p. 157.

days, the doctors ordered cords to be brought to bind Joseph fast to a bedstead, but to this he objected. Next it was proposed that he be given brandy or wine to deaden the pain, but again Joseph refused. Said he, "No, I will not touch one particle of liquor, neither will I be tied down; but I will tell you what I will do—I will have my father sit on the bed and hold me in his arms, and then I will do whatever is necessary in order to have the bone taken out."

After his mother had been sent from the room, "the surgeons commenced operating by boring into the bone of his leg, first on one side of the bone where it was affected, then on the other side, after which they broke the infected parts off with a pair of forceps or pincers." Several pieces were removed. The operation left young Joseph pale, weak, and perspiring; but it was successful in checking the malady, and he soon began to recover.[52]

While he was en route to Washington, in 1839, the coachman of the stage in which he and others were riding stepped into a public house to take his grog. Somehow the horses took fright and ran down a steep hill at full speed. The passengers were immediately panic-stricken, some of them to the point of hysteria. One woman endeavored to throw her baby out of the window but was restrained from doing so by the Prophet. Some men attempted to jump out. Coaches in those days were great, cumbersome things: high decked-over tops, with railings, where mail sacks and trunks were carried, and sometimes passengers rode up there. The seat for the driver was in front, so high that the top of the coach formed but little support for his back. After quieting the passengers somewhat, the Prophet opened the door, secured a hold on the side of the speeding coach, and succeeded in getting into the driver's seat. After

---

[52]Smith, op. cit., pp. 54-58.

the racing horses had carried their frightened cargo some two or three miles, he was able to rein them up.

Joseph's actions were spoken of in the highest terms of commendation as "one of the most daring and heroic deeds, and no language could express the gratitude of the passengers." There were members of Congress present who even proposed mentioning the incident to that body with the intention of rewarding "such conduct by some public act." But when they inquired concerning their rescuer's name and were informed that he was Joseph Smith the Mormon Prophet, their praise subsided, and Joseph heard no more of their proposals.[53]

In the effort to kidnap Joseph Smith which was mentioned before, he again demonstrated his courage and fearlessness. His enemies thrust loaded pistols into his side with the oath, "G— d— you, if you say another word I will shoot you, by G—." But the Prophet calmly replied, "Shoot away; I am not afraid of your pistols."[54] By his courage he strengthened his brethren and carried them through trials and difficulties that might otherwise have been insurmountable. When a mob force of some 3,500 was approaching Far West, shortly before the Saints were driven from Missouri, Lieutenant-Colonel George M. Hinkle, commander of the Mormon forces, ordered a retreat. "Retreat!" exclaimed Joseph Smith. "Why, where in the name of God shall we go?" Then turning to the men around him he said, "Boys, follow me!" A band of about two hundred men went with him out on the open prairie to face the force of 3,500. While they prepared for a showdown, the Prophet sent word to the enemy by one of their messengers, saying, "Go tell your general for me that if he does not immediately withdraw his men, I will send them

[53]History of the Church, IV, pp. 23-24; Young Woman's Journal, II, p. 77.
[54]History of the Church, V, pp. 440-441.

to hell!" The mob charged only to retreat in disorder and confusion before reaching the Mormon lines.[55] At another time the threat was reversed, and a mob threatened to send the Saints to hell. But the Prophet rejoined, "If they do we will turn the devils out and make a heaven out of it."[56] His advice to George A. Smith is classic. "Never be discouraged," said he to his cousin; "if I were sunk in the lowest pit of Nova Scotia, with the Rocky Mountains piled on me, I would hang on, exercise faith, and keep up good courage, and I would come out on top."[57]

Warren Waste, reputedly the strongest man in the Western Reserve, witnessed a test of the Prophet's strength, will, and courage. As one of a mob that dragged Joseph from his bed in the middle of the night, Waste had boasted that he alone could take the Prophet out of the house. But as he and others were undertaking their fiendish designs, Waste had hold of one foot when the Prophet gave him a kick that sent him sprawling off the steps. The imprint made in the ground by his head and shoulders could still be seen the next morning. With his boastful spirit cooled, Waste recovered himself and cried, "Do not let him touch the ground, or he will run over the whole of us." He afterwards said that the Prophet was "the most powerful man" he had ever had hold of in his life.

The Prophet was then beaten and choked into insensibility by the combined strength of the mob; he recovered to find himself being taken some forty rods from the house toward a meadow. There the mob tore off his night clothes, stretched him upon a board, and tantalized him in the most

---

[55]As reported by John Taylor. Cited in *Stories about Joseph Smith the Prophet*, pp. 72-73.

[56]*History of the Church*, V, p. 517.

[57]Cited in John Henry Evans, *Joseph Smith an American Prophet* (New York, 1940), p. 9.

insulting and brutal manner.[58]   He was beaten, scratched, and finally covered with tar and feathers.   One mobocrat fell upon him and, while kicking and clawing his body, cried, "D— you, this is the way the Holy Ghost falls upon you."   Another tried to force a tar paddle into his mouth and another a phial said to contain nitric acid, but it was broken against his teeth.   One of his front teeth was also broken, thereafter causing a slight whistle when he spoke. So powerful was this acid that the grass was killed where it spilled upon the ground.

Despite this treatment and the fact that he spent the remaining part of the night cleaning tar and feathers from his body and treating his wounds, the Prophet fulfilled a preaching engagement the next morning.   Among the listeners were some who had so cruelly assaulted him a few hours before.[59]

A few years later, as the Saints were being driven from Missouri and the Prophet was imprisoned at Richmond, William E. McLellin went to the sheriff and asked permission to flog the prisoner.   McLellin, a large and active man, was an apostate who had once been a member of the Quorum of the Twelve.   Permission was granted on condition that Joseph would fight.   To this the Prophet agreed on condition that his irons were to be taken off. McLellin then refused to fight unless he could have a club, to which Joseph consented; but the sheriff would not allow them to fight on such unequal terms.[60]

The Prophet's sense of security amid turmoil and persecution was founded largely in his faith in God and in

---

[58]Their intention was to emasculate him, and a Dr. Dennison was there to perform the operation, but the doctor's courage failed at the last moment and he refused.

[59]*Millennial Star*, XXVI, pp. 834-835; J. D., XI, p. 5; XXVI, p. 21; B. H. Roberts, *Comprehensive History of the Church*, I, pp. 280-282.

[60]*Millennial Star*, XXVI, p. 808.

his awareness of the divine mission to which he had been called. Shortly after he and others were taken captive in Missouri, he arose one morning and whispered cheerfully and confidently to his fellow prisoners, "Be of good cheer, brethren; the word of the Lord came to me last night that our lives should be given us, and that whatever we may suffer during captivity, not one of our lives should be taken."[61] This assurance buoyed up the brethren throughout the ordeals of their captivity. When Parley P. Pratt found an opportunity to escape which, while allowing him his freedom, would have jeopardized the lives of the other prisoners, he thought of the Prophet's promise and returned to his imprisoned brethren.[62]

Some time after his escape from Missouri, Joseph Smith was forced into hiding by enemies who sought his life. His companion in exile, William Taylor, inquired, "Brother Joseph, don't you get frightened when all those hungry wolves are after you?" The Prophet's reply again revealed the source of the security he manifested throughout his life. Said he, "No, I am not afraid; the Lord said he would protect me, and I have full confidence in His word."[63]

The Prophet's courage was combined with supreme integrity. Lorenzo Snow said, "There never was a man that possessed a higher degree of integrity and more devotedness to the interests of mankind than the Prophet Joseph Smith."[64] When Zion's Camp made the arduous journey from Kirtland to Missouri, in 1834, Joseph Smith demonstrated on many occasions what L. O. Littlefield termed as his "natural and inspired characteristic" of integrity. Littlefield said of him, "It is due his memory for

[61]*Autobiography of Parley Parker Pratt* (Salt Lake City, 1950), p. 192.
[62]*Ibid.*, pp. 192-197.
[63]*Young Women's Journal*, XVII, p. 548.
[64]*Conference Report*, October, 1897, p. 64.

me to here place on record the fact that I never, in that camp or during the trials of his later life, saw Joseph Smith the Prophet falter or shrink from the performance of any duty or undertaking that the Lord had commanded or inaugurated."[65]   Moses Martin wrote in his *Journal,* "The road was so bad that we twice during the day had to unhitch our teams from our wagons and draw them by hand.   Here I saw the Prophet wade in mud over the tops of his boot legs and help draw the wagons out."[66]   Another member of the camp noted other similar experiences and bore a like testimony, stating, "Zion's Camp, in passing through the State of Indiana, had to cross very bad swamps, consequently we had to attach ropes to the wagons to help them through, and the Prophet was the first man at the rope in his bare feet.   This was characteristic of him in all times of difficulty."[67]   George A. Smith also wrote concerning that journey:

> The Prophet Joseph took a full share of the fatigues of the entire journey.   In addition to the care of providing for the Camp and presiding over it, he walked most of the time and had a full proportion of blistered, bloody and sore feet, which was the natural result of walking from 25 to 40 miles a day in a hot season of the year.   But during the entire trip he never uttered a murmur or complaint, while most of the men in the Camp complained to him of sore toes, blistered feet, long drives, scanty supply of provisions, poor quality of bread, bad corn dodger, frouzey butter, strong honey, maggotty bacon and cheese, etc., even a dog could not bark at some men without their murmuring at Joseph.   If they had to camp with bad water it would nearly cause rebellion, yet we were the Camp of Zion, and many of us were

---

[65]*Juvenile Instructor,* XXVII, pp. 223-224.
[66]*Journal History,* May 20, 1834.
[67]Statement by John M. Chidester, *Juvenile Instructor,* XXVII, p. 151.

prayerless, thoughtless, careless, heedless, foolish
or devilish and yet we did not know it. Joseph
had to bear with us and tutor us, like children.
There were many, however, in the Camp who
never murmured and who were always ready and
willing to do as our leaders desired.[68]

Said George Q. Cannon with reference to the Prophet's integrity, as manifested throughout his life of tribulation and persecution:

> Think of what he passed through! Think of
> his afflictions, and think of his dauntless character!
> Did any one ever see him falter? Did any one ever
> see him flinch? Did any one ever see any lack in
> him of the power necessary to enable him to stand
> with dignity in the midst of his enemies, or lacking
> in dignity in the performance of his duties as a
> servant of the living God? God gave him peculiar
> power in this respect. He was filled with integrity
> to God; with such integrity as was not known
> among men. He was like an angel of God among
> them. Notwithstanding all that he had to endure,
> and the peculiar circumstances in which he was
> so often placed, and the great responsibility that
> weighed constantly upon him, he never faltered;
> the feeling of fear or trembling never crossed him
> —at least he never exhibited it in his feelings or
> actions. God sustained him to the very last,
> and was with him, and bore him off triumphant
> even in his death.[69]

Men with such a rare blend of admirable qualities as
Joseph Smith possessed seldom appear on the scene of
history. His physical appearance was commanding and
inviting to look upon. His personality was charming and
magnetic. While he possessed the strength of a giant, he

---

[68]George A. Smith's *Journal*, June 25, 1834.
[69]*J. D.*, XXIII, p. 362.

had the agility of a chipmunk. Yet he was gentle and easy
to approach, even by those in lowly stations. His keen
penetrating eye was ever alert and discerning; and when
truth was revealed, his courage and integrity in following
its course knew no bounds. Such traits of character, with
others yet to be discussed, caused Joseph Smith to stand
out as a man among men and contributed to his stature as
a latter-day prophet of God.

II.

Other Personality Traits of the Prophet

Of all the men Josiah Quincy ever met in his role as traveler and public servant, there were two only who stood out in his mind as possessing that "sort of personal power" that immediately attracts the attention of others and commands their allegiance. Those two were Elisha R. Potter of Rhode Island, a member of the United States Congress, and Joseph Smith, the Mormon Prophet. The resemblance of the two men was not basically physical, though both were commanding figures. Said Quincy:

> The likeness was not such as would be recognized in a picture, but rather one that would be felt in a grave emergency. Of all men I have met, these two seemed best endowed with the kingly faculty which directs, as by intrinsic right, the feeble or confused souls who are looking for guidance.[1]

In this light Quincy compared the personal characteristics of these two men. Of the Congressman from Rhode Island, he said:

> Mr. Potter was one of the men who carry about them a surplus of vital energy, to relieve the wants of others. The absurd inquiry whether life were worth living never suggested itself in his presence. . . . He was said to have been a

[1]Quincy, *op. cit.,* pp. 277-279, 381.

LIEUT. GEN. JOSEPH SMITH,
Mormon Prophet.

Joseph Smith.

    Portrait of the Prophet Joseph Smith as Lieutenant General of the Nauvoo Legion. The painter of this, one of the earliest portraits of the Prophet, is unknown.

blacksmith in his early days, and the occupation probably confirmed his robust frame and gave his cheery self-reliance a substantial physical basis. Mr. Potter seemed to carry about with him a certain homespun certificate of authority, which made it natural for lesser men to accept his conclusions.[2]

The same could be said of Joseph Smith. Both were men who received "from nature the best credentials." Quincy wrote:

When I made the acquaintance of the Mormon prophet I was haunted with a provoking sense of having known him before; or, at least, of having known some one whom he greatly resembled. And then followed a painful groping and peering "in the dark backward and abysm of time," in search of the figure that was provokingly undiscoverable. At last the Washington of 1826 came up before me, and the form of Elisha R. Potter thrust itself through the gorges of memory. Yes, that was the man I was seeking; yet the resemblance, after all, could scarcely be called physical, and I am loath to borrow the word "impressional" from the vocabulary of spirit mediums. Both were of commanding appearance, men whom it seemed natural to obey. Wide as were the differences between the lives and characters of these Americans, there emanated from each of them a certain peculiar moral stress and compulsion which I have never felt in the presence of others of their countrymen.[3]

Among other things, Quincy wrote in his essay of the Prophet's quick wit. As he and others finished dining in the Mansion House at Nauvoo, the request was made that Joseph Smith preach to the group. To this request

---

[2]*Idem.*
[3]*Idem.*

he readily complied, emphasizing in his discourse that baptism for the remission of sins was essential to salvation.
"Stop!" interrupted a Methodist minister who was present
among the listeners. "What do you say to the case of the
penitent thief?"

"What do you mean?" inquired the Prophet.

The minister explained, "You know our Savior said
to the thief, 'This day shalt thou be with me in paradise,'
which shows he could not have been baptized before his
admission."

To this the Prophet quipped, "How do you know he
wasn't baptized before he became a thief?" When the
spontaneous outburst of mirth that followed had subsided,
he continued on a more serious note, "But that is not the
true answer. In the original Greek, as this gentleman
[turning to Quincy] will inform you, the word that has
been translated paradise means simply a place of departed
spirits. To that place the penitent thief was conveyed, and
there, doubtless, he received [vicariously] the baptism
necessary for his admission to the heavenly kingdom."[4]

While the Prophet escorted his visitors about the city,
the minister continued the contest on one issue after another. As they stopped in a beautiful grove, Joseph commented, pointing to a platform and a number of seats,
"When the weather permits we hold our services in this
place; but shall cease to do so when the Temple is finished."

The minister remarked with a note of sarcasm, "I
suppose none but Mormon preachers are allowed in Nauvoo."

"On the contrary," replied the Prophet, "I shall be
very happy to have you address my people next Sunday,
and I will insure you a most attentive congregation."

4*Ibid.*, pp. 391-392.

"What! do you mean that I may say anything I please and that you will make no reply?" inquired the minister.

To this the Mormon leader replied, "You may certainly say anything you please; but I must reserve the right of adding a word or two, if I judge best. I promise to speak of you in the most respectful manner."

As they rode on the dispute continued. "Come," said the Prophet as he slapped his antagonist on the knee to emphasize his production of a triumphant text, "if you can't argue better than that, you shall say all you want to say to my people and I will promise to hold my tongue. For there's not a Mormon among them who would need any assistance to answer you."

The minister later sought to even things up by referring to some point of doctrine which he considered erroneous. "Why, I told my congregation the other Sunday that they might as well believe Joe Smith as such theology as that," he declared.

"Did you say Joe Smith in a sermon?" inquired the Mormon leader.

"Of course I did. Why not?" rejoined the minister.

The Prophet's reply was given with a quiet superiority that was overwhelming: "Considering only the day and the place, it would have been more respectful to have said Lieutenant-General Joseph Smith."

"Clearly," Quincy concluded, "the worthy minister was no match for the head of the Mormon church."[5]

Joseph Smith was noted for his frank, open, unassuming, forthright, and jovial manner. Parley P. Pratt wrote of his first meeting with him, stating, "He received me with a hearty welcome, and with that frank and kind manner so

---

[5]*Ibid.*, pp. 392-393.

universal with him in after years."[6]   Wilford Woodruff
gave a similar account, in reporting a meeting with the
Prophet: "Joseph was frank, open and familiar as usual,
and our rejoicing was great."[7]   Helen Mar Whitney related the following incident which gives a similar picture
of these features of the Prophet's character:

> It was near the first of June, 1843 . . . that the
> Prophet called and invited him [Heber C. Kim-
> ball] to ride with him and William Clayton, his
> private clerk. . . . I [as Kimball's daughter] was
> also invited to go along. As we drove up the river
> a steamer was just landing, and a number of
> strange gentlemen came ashore, who seemed to
> have quite a curiosity to see the Prophet. He got
> out, and in his warm and genial way, gave each
> of them a cordial shake of the hand. As the
> carriage was about starting away, one of them
> came up and . . . requested the privilege of riding.
> After going a few rods the carriage was stopped
> for him to get out. He wished to have it to say
> that he had ridden with Joseph Smith, whom they
> styled the "American Mohamet."[8]

After frequent conversations with Joseph Smith, a
visitor at Nauvoo described him as "a sensible, intelligent,
companionable, and gentlemanly man."[9]   Said a United
States Congressman after hearing him speak:

> He is not an educated man; but he is a plain,
> sensible, strong-minded man. Everything he says
> is said in a manner to leave an impression that he
> is sincere. There is no levity, no fanaticism, no
> want of dignity in his deportment.[10]

---

[6]*Journal History*, September, 1830.
[7]*Ibid.*, May 3, 1839.
[8]Whitney, *op. cit.*, XI, p. 58.
[9]*Columbus Advocate*, Columbus, Ohio. Reprinted in *Millennial Star*, III
(June, 1842), p. 25; *History of the Church*, IV, p. 566.
[10]*The Historical Record, op. cit.*, p. 476.

Orson Spencer described the Prophet as follows:

... he is kind and obliging; pitiful and courte-
ous; as far from dissimulation as any man; frank
and loquacious to all men, friends or foes. He
seems to employ no studied effort to guard himself against misrepresentation, but often leaves
himself exposed to misconstructions by those who
watch for faults. He is remarkably cheerful for
one who has seen well-tried friends martyred
around him, and felt the inflictions of calumny—
the vexations of lawsuits—the treachery of inti-
mates—and multiplied violent attempts upon his
person and life, together with the cares of much
business. His influence, after which you inquire,
is very great. His friends are as ardently attached
to him as his enemies are violently opposed. . . .
That lurking fear and suspicion that he may become a dictator or despot, gradually gives place to
confidence and fondness, as believers become acquainted with him.[11]

As witnessed by Spencer and others, the Prophet
possessed "that strong comradeship that made such a bond
of brotherliness with those who were his companions in
civil and military life, and in which he reached men's souls,
and appealed most forcibly to their friendship and loyalty."[12]
But Joseph was not one to attract the loyalty, consideration,
and friendship of others without a full return of like expressions on his part. His consideration for others began at
his family circle and extended to his friends and associates,
and from there it expanded to the whole of mankind. As
letters written when his enemies forced him into hiding bear

---

[11]Orson Spencer, *Letters Exhibiting the Most Prominent Doctrines of the
Church of Jesus Christ of Latter-day Saints*, 6th ed. (Salt Lake City, 1891), p. 26.
See *Millennial Star* (August 31, 1861), pp. 560-578, for a similar statement by
William Clayton, another close associate of the Prophet.
[12]Statement by Emmeline B. Wells, *Young Woman's Journal*, XVI, pp.
555-556.

witness, isolation from family and friends was to him almost unbearable. Several references in his *Journal* reveal his genuine concern for his family. For example, while away on a journey he wrote, "O Lord! keep us and my family safe, until I return unto them."[13] Later, he recorded, "I found my family all well. The Lord be praised for this blessing."[14] The following day he noted, "Remained at home and had great joy with my family."[15]

Among his associates, it was the Prophet's "ambition to be one with the humble, and there was no feeling of ag-grandisement with him."[16] He was "always approachable to the humblest of his acquaintances"[17] and ever expressed genuine concern for the interests of others. As persecution commenced against the Saints in Missouri, he prayed, "O my God, have mercy on my brethren in Zion, for Christ's sake, Amen."[18] When the Saints had been driven from Missouri and began to settle in Illinois, Joseph went to Quincy, where "he visited around from house to house among the Saints to see how they were situated, and gave words of strength and encouragement to them."[19] When informed some time later that a brother who lived some distance from Nauvoo had had his house burned down, nearly everyone present expressed sympathy for the man. But Joseph put his hand in his pocket, took out five dollars, and said: "I feel sorry for this brother to the amount of five dollars; how much do you feel sorry?"[20] On another occasion a group of people, as guests of the Prophet, took a ride with him on the *Maid of Iowa,* a boat that he and others had purchased while in

[13]*Journal History,* January 16, 1834.
[14]*Ibid.,* March 28, 1834.
[15]*Ibid.,* March 29, 1834.
[16]"The Life Story of Mosiah Lyman Hancock," typewritten copy, Brigham Young University Library, p. 24.
[17]Statement by Jane Snyder Richards, *Young Woman's Journal,* XVI, p. 550.
[18]*Journal History,* January 16, 1834.
[19]*Young Woman's Journal,* XVI, p. 557.
[20]*Juvenile Instructor,* XXVII, p. 641.

Nauvoo. They were caught in a severe rainstorm, and some became ill from exposure. According to Helen Mar Whitney, "The Prophet, who was noted for his tender sympathies towards the afflicted, could not rest until he went around and informed himself of the condition of each one who had accompanied him to Quincy, and offered advice and some he administered to."[21]   The following story, told by Mary Frost Adams, also illustrates the consideration Joseph Smith had for others:

> While he was acting as mayor of the city, a colored man named Anthony was arrested for selling liquor on Sunday, contrary to law. He pleaded that the reason he had done so was that he might raise the money to purchase the freedom of a dear child held as a slave in a Southern State. . . . Joseph said,
>
> "I am sorry, Anthony, but the law must be observed, and we will have to impose a fine."
>
> The next day Brother Joseph presented Anthony with a fine horse, directing him to sell it, and use the money obtained for the purchase of the child.[22]

Joseph Smith was "partial to a well supplied table";[23] and here, too, he desired his family and friends to be with him. While conversing on the topic of food with William W. Phelps, Joseph remarked that when he wanted only a little bread and milk, his wife, Emma, would load the table with all kinds of good things to eat.

As Emma came into the room, Phelps commented, "You must do as Bonaparte did—have a little table, just large enough for the victuals you want yourself."

[21]Whitney, op. cit.
[22]Young Woman's Journal, XVII, p. 538.
[23]Johnson, op. cit., p. 4.

To this comment Emma retorted, "Mr. Smith is a bigger man than Bonaparte: he can never eat without his friends."[24]

The Prophet's consideration for others was founded in charity. Whether it was a bounteous table or the last crust in his possession made little difference. Those in need were welcome to share with him. Said he:

> If any man is hungry, let him come to me, and I will feed him at my table. If any are hungry or naked . . . come and tell me and I will divide with them to the last morsel; and then if the man is not satisfied, I will kick his backside.[25]

Socially, Joseph Smith was "an ideal of affability."[26] He "always had a smile for his friends and was always cheerful,"[27] Mosiah Hancock remarked. Said L. O. Littlefield, "With his most familiar friends he was social, conversational and often indulged in harmless jokes."[28] A visitor to Nauvoo, after meeting Joseph Smith, wrote:

> He is a jolly fellow, and according to his view he is one of the last persons on earth whom God would have raised up as a prophet or priest, he is so diametrically opposite to that which he ought to be in order to merit the titles or to act in such offices. Among others he is very sociable, cheerful, kind and obliging, and very hospitable.[29]

William Taylor, who was the Prophet's companion for some time in 1842, also wrote:

> It is impossible for me to express my feelings

[24]History of the Church, VI, pp. 165-166.
[25]Ibid., V, p. 286.
[26]Statement by Jane Snyder Richards, Young Woman's Journal, XVI, p. 550.
[27]"The Life Story of Mosiah Hancock," p. 3.
[28]Statement by L. O. Littlefield, Juvenile Insturctor, XXVII, pp. 56-57.
[29]History of the Church, V, p. 432.

in regard to this period of my life. I have never
known the same joy and satisfaction in the com-
panionship of any other person, man or woman,
that I felt with him, the man who had conversed
with the Almighty. He was always the most companionable and lovable of men—cheerful and
jovial.[30]

Joseph Smith went out of his way to encourage wholesome fun and amusement. While out raising money to free
his friend, Orrin Porter Rockwell, from an unjust imprisonment in Missouri, the Prophet came to a large crowd of
young men occupied in wrestling. Among them was a
bully from the neighboring town of La Harpe, Hancock
County, Illinois, who had thrown everyone who wrestled
with him. Said Calvin W. Moore, who was present:

When Joseph came to the crowd he told them
what he wanted, passed around the hat, raised
what money he could and then went into the ring
to take part with the young men and boys in their
games. So he was invited to wrestle with this
bully. The man was eager to have a tussel with
the Prophet, so Joseph stepped forward and took
hold of the man. The first pass he made Joseph
whirled him round and took him by the collar and
seat of his trousers and walked out to a ditch and
threw him in it. Then, taking him by the arm, he
helped him up and patted him on the back and
said: "You must not mind this. When I am with
the boys I make all the fun I can for them."[31]

It would be hard to be angry with a man like that, even
in defeat.

---

[30]*Young Woman's Journal,* XVII, p. 548. Said Wandle Mace of the Prophet's
playful nature:
    "He often tried to get me to wrestle with him. I never could. I was a strong
man as well as he was. Often when we met and shook hands he would pull me to
him for a wrestle."—Mace, *op. cit.,* pp. 97-98.
[31]*Juvenile Instructor,* XXVII, p. 255.

Of Joseph's sociability, Benjamin F. Johnson explained, "When with us, there was no lack of amusement; for with jokes, games, etc., he was ready to provoke merriment, one phase of which was matching couplets in rhyme."[32] Johnson gave the following picture of the Prophet on another occasion:

> As a son, he was nobility itself, in love and honor to his parents; as a brother he was loving and true, even unto death; as a husband and father, his devotion to wives and children stopped only at idolatry. His life's greatest motto after "God and His Kingdom" was that of "wives, children and friends." . . .
>
> As a companion, socially, he was highly endowed; was kind, generous, mirth loving, and at times, even convivial. . . . Jokes, rebuses, matching couplets in rhymes, etc., were not uncommon. But to call for the singing of one or more of his favorite songs was more frequent. Of those, "Wives, Children and Friends," "Battle of River Russen," "Soldier's Tear," "Soldier's Dream," and "Last Rose of Summer" were most common. And yet, although so social and even convivial at times, he would allow no arrogance or undue liberties, and criticisms, even by his associates, were rarely acceptable, and contradictions would rouse in him the lion at once, for by no one of his fellows would he be superseded.[33]

George Q. Cannon was another who knew Joseph Smith and who gave a description of his personal characteristics and magnetic powers. Cannon wrote:

> His majesty of air was natural, not studied. Though full of personal and prophetic dignity

---

[32]Benjamin F. Johnson, *My Life's Review* (Independence, Mo., 1947), pp. 92-93.

[33]Johnson, "An Interesting Letter," p. 4.

whenever occasion demanded, he could at other times unbend and be as happy and unconventional as a boy. This was one of his most striking characteristics.

But whether engaging in manly sport, during hours of relaxation, or proclaiming words of wisdom in pulpit or grove, he was ever the leader. His magnetism was masterful, and his heroic qualities won universal admiration. Where he moved, all classes were forced to recognize in him the man of power. Strangers journeying to see him from a distance, knew him the moment their eyes beheld his person.[34]

While playful and even convivial, the Prophet's natural tastes were pitched at a high and refined level. Emmeline B. Wells said of him, "He possessed . . . the innate refinement that one finds in the born poet, or in the most highly cultivated intellectual and poetic nature; and this extraordinary temperament and force combined is something of a miracle and can scarcely be accounted for except as a 'heavenly mystery' of the 'higher sort.' "[35]   Newel Knight also referred to the superior gifts and to the refined endowments that were blended with the elements of playfulness and consideration for others in Joseph Smith, even during his boyhood:

> His noble deportment, his faithfulness, and his kind address, could not fail to win the esteem of those who had the pleasure of his acquaintance. One thing I will mention, which seemed to be a peculiar characteristic with him in all his boyish sports and amusements. I never knew anyone to gain advantage over him and yet he was always kind and kept the good will of his playmates.[36]

---

[34]Cannon, op. cit., p. xxvi.
[35]Young Woman's Journal, XVI, pp. 555-556.
[36]Jesse William Knight, The Jesse Knight Family: Jesse Knight, His Forebears and Family (Salt Lake City, 1940), pp. 9-10.

Joseph was noted particularly for demonstrating "his childlike love and familiarity with children, and he never seemed to feel that he was losing any of his honor or dignity in doing so." Often, when he "heard the cry of a child he would rush out of the house to see if it was harmed."[37] "He was so fond of children," said Joseph F. Smith, "that he would go far out of his way to speak to a little one."[38] One of the Prophet's young acquaintances later reported that he was a "great favorite among the children," and added, "I have known him many times, to stop as he passed the playgrounds, when we were out of school, and shake hands with the girls, and play a game of marbles with the boys."[39] L. O. Littlefield said:

> He was naturally fond of the young—especially the little children. He did not like to pass a child, however small, without speaking to it. He has been known to actually cross a street if he saw a child alone on the opposite side, to speak to it or to inquire if it had lost its way.[40]

Littlefield, who, as a youth, accompanied Zion's Camp to Missouri, later cited a case in point which occurred while they were encamped at the Salt River:

> While there the men were paraded outside of the camp for exercise and instruction. This was an unpleasant feature for me, as I was too young and too small of stature to act with the men. This created within me, as I remember, some lonesome reflections. I sat down upon a rock where the men were passing, the better to observe their movements. While thus seated, the Prophet Joseph

[37]Whitney, op. cit., p. 146.
[38]The Improvement Era, XXI (December, 1917), p. 167. See also Anderson, op. cit.
[39]"A Biographical Sketch of the Life of Mary Jane Lytle Little," in Mormon Diaries, XVI, p. 90.
[40]Juvenile Instructor, XXVII, p. 109.

Smith, who happened to be passing by in quite a hurry, noticed me.

He stepped to where I sat alone. It might have been my isolated position that attracted him. I knew not the motive; but that man, who to me appeared so good and so godlike, really halted in his hurry to notice me—only a little boy. Placing one of his hands upon my head, he said: "Well, bub, is there no place for you?"

This recognition from the man who I then knew was a Prophet of God created within me a tumult of emotions. I could make him no reply. My young heart was filled with joy to me unspeakable. He passed on and left me in my lonely attitude, for he was then in quite a hurry to accomplish something pertaining to the movements of the men which could not be delayed.[41]

The Mormon Prophet fully exemplified the teachings and example of Christ in his conduct toward little children. Mosiah Hancock said, "It was the disposition of the Prophet when he saw little children in the mud to take them up in his arms and wash the mud from their bare feet with his handkerchief."[42]   Not only did he minister to their needs but he also blessed them, as Joseph F. Smith later reported, saying, "He never saw a child but he desired to take it up and bless it and many he did so bless, taking them in his arms and upon his knee."[43]   An early convert also recalled:

In Kirtland when wagon loads of grown people and children came in from the country to meeting, Joseph would make his way to as many of the wagons as he could and cordially shake the hand of each person.   Every child and young babe in the company were especially noticed by him and tenderly taken by the hand, with his kind words

[41]*Idem.*
[42]"The Life Story of Mosiah Lyman Hancock," p. 3.
[43]*The Improvement Era,* XXI (December, 1917), p. 167.

and blessings. He loved innocence and purity, and he seemed to find it in the greatest perfection with the prattling child.[44]

"I never saw another man like Joseph," said John W. Hess, as he spoke of the "kindness and simplicity" of his nature. "There was something heavenly and angelic in his looks that I never witnessed in the countenance of any other person." The Prophet stayed for thirteen days at the Hess home, after which John, then a lad of fourteen, related that he "became very much attached to him, and learned to love him more dearly than any other person" he ever met, his father and mother not excepted.[45]

The Prophet's love and compassion were universal. "He manifested a greatness of soul which I had never seen in any other man," declared Wilford Woodruff.[46] Friendship and love were ruling principles in his life. In exhorting the Saints to express true kindness and love unto all mankind, he explained, "Friendship is like Brother [Theodore] Turley in his blacksmith shop welding iron to iron; it unites the human family with its happy influence."[47] Again he declared, "Friendship is one of the grand fundamental principles of 'Mormonism'; [it is designed] to revolutionize and civilize the world, and cause wars and contentions to cease and men to become friends and brothers."[48]

In the presidential campaign of 1844, Joseph Smith sought to raise the nation and the world to the standard of friendship and love. In his "Views of the Powers and Policy of the Government of the United States," he declared that

---

[44]Statement by Louisa Y. Littlefield, *Juvenile Instructor*, XXVII, p. 24.
[45]*Juvenile Instructor*, XXVII, p. 302.
[46]*J. D.*, VII, p. 101.
[47]*History of the Church*, V, p. 517.
[48]*Ibid.*

Open, frank, candid decorum to all men, in
this boasted land of liberty, would beget esteem,
confidence, union, and love; and the neighbor from
any state or from any country, of whatever color,
clime or tongue, could rejoice when he put his foot
on the sacred soil of freedom, and exclaim, the
very name of *"America"* is fraught with "friendship!"   Oh, then, create confidence, restore freedom, break down slavery, banish imprisonment for
debt, and be in love, fellowship and peace with all
the world![49]

Again he declared, *"Come,* yea, come, Texas; come
Mexico, come Canada; and come, all the world: let us be
brethren, let us be one great family, and let there be a
universal peace."[50]

The principle of love was in large measure the secret
of Joseph Smith's power and influence.   Said he:

Sectarian priests cry out concerning me, and
ask, "Why is it this babbler gains so many followers, and retains them?"   I answer, It is because
I possess the principle of love.   All I can offer the
world is a good heart and a good hand.

The Saints can testify whether I am willing
to lay down my life for my brethren.[51]

Several incidents and expressions attest to the truth-
fulness of the Prophet's statement.   William Clayton wrote
to a friend, "The more I am with him, the more I love him;
the more I know of him, the more confidence I have in
him."[52]   After journeying to Harmony, Pennsylvania, to
see the Prophet, Newel Knight reported, "We had a happy
meeting.   It truly gave me joy to again behold his face."[53]

---

[49]*Ibid.,* VI, pp. 205-206.
[50]*Ibid.,* p. 208.
[51]*Ibid.,* V, p. 498.
[52]*Millennial Star,* August 1, 1842.
[53]*Journal History,* August, 1830.

When George Laub returned from a journey, "longing to see the Prophet," he wrote, "I then had the opportunity of striking glad hands with him and my heart leaped in me for joy, for I had greater affection towards him than for any person on earth."[54]   Another wrote that he "felt willing" to lay down his life because of his love for the Prophet.[55] Said Enoch E. Dodge, "Every Saint who knew him loved him, and would have been willing to lay down his life for him if it had been necessary."[56]   Another said, "As an evidence of the admiration in which he was held by his people, let me say that it was the common custom for men, women and children, alike, to flock to the road side and salute him as he passed along."[57]   In the words of Mary Alice Lambert,

> The love the Saints had for him was inexpressible. They would willingly have laid down their lives for him. If he was to talk, every task would be laid aside that they might listen to his words. He was not an ordinary man. Saints and sinners alike felt and recognized a power and influence which he carried with him. It was impossible to meet him and not be impressed by the strength of his personality and influence.

In May, 1844, he went to the stone shops where the men were working on the Nauvoo Temple and blessed them, each man by the power of

---

[54]"Diary of George Laub, 1814-1880," typewritten copy in Brigham Young University Library, I, p. 17. The writer has corrected misspelled words and added punctuation in this quote.

[55]*Juvenile Instructor,* XXVII, p. 66. In December, 1842, Phineas H. Young wrote from Tiffin, Seneca County, Ohio, to Willard Richards, in Nauvoo:
" . . . I long to see the day when I can again visit my brethren and see the Lord's Prophet and hear the words of life sweetly distilling from his lips. . . .
"Give my love to Brother Joseph, when you see him. Tell him I would come to the Rocky Mountains to see him, and fight my way through an army of wild cats or Missouri wolves and live on skunks the whole journey, if necessary."— *Journal History,* December 14, 1842.

[56]*Young Woman's Journal,* XVII, p. 544. William Taylor added:
"Much has been said of his geniality and personal magnetism. I was a witness of this—people, old and young, loved him and trusted him instinctively."—*Ibid.,* p. 548.

[57]*Ibid.,* XVI, p. 550.

his Priesthood.   Brother Lambert (whom I afterward married) he gathered right into his arms and
blessed, and it was ever his testimony that he was
thrilled from head to foot by that blessing.[58]

George A. Smith also reported that while conversing
with the Prophet on one occasion, "Joseph wrapped his
arms around me and pressed me to his bosom and said,
'George A., I love you as I do my own life.' "   With a deep-
felt emotion that choked his words, the latter replied, "I
hope, Brother Joseph, that my whole life and actions will
ever prove my feelings and affections toward you."[59]   That
same love for the Prophet Joseph dominated the life of
Brigham Young.   In meeting the Prophet, following his
escape from Missouri, Brigham wrote that it was "one of
the most joyful scenes of my life" to "strike hands" with
him again.[60]   Brigham later declared, "I honor and revere
the name of Joseph Smith.   I delight to hear it; I love it.
I love his doctrine."[61]   And with his last breath on earth
he whispered, "Joseph! Joseph! Joseph!"[62]

Shortly after the Prophet and others, including Lyman
Wight, were betrayed into the hands of the mob forces in
Missouri, General Moses Wilson came to Lyman Wight
seeking for testimony against Joseph Smith, to be used
in his trial by "court-martial."

"Wight," he said, "we have nothing against
you, only that you are associated with Joe Smith.
He is our enemy and a d——d rascal, and would
take any plan he could to kill us. You are a d——d
fine fellow.   If you will come out and swear
against him we will spare your life, and give you

---

[58]*Ibid.*, p. 554.
[59]George A. Smith's *Journal*, under 1843. No other date given. Church
Historian's Office, Salt Lake City, Utah.
[60]*Journal History*, May 3, 1839.
[61]*J. D.*, XIII, p. 216.
[62]See Daryl Chase, *Joseph the Prophet* (Salt Lake City, 1944), p. 22.

any office you want; and if you don't you will be shot to-morrow at nine."

"General Wilson," the redoubtable Colonel answered, "you are entirely mistaken in your man, both in regard to myself and Joseph Smith. Joseph Smith is not an enemy to mankind. He is not your enemy. In fact, he is as good a friend as you have. For had it not been for Joseph Smith, you would have been in hell long ago, and I would have sent you there myself by cutting your throat, and no other man but Joseph Smith could have prevented me. You may thank him for being alive. And now, if you will give me the boys I brought from Diahman yesterday, I will whip your whole army."

Wilson was silent for a moment. Then he said, "Wight, you're a strange man. But if you do not accept my proposal, you will be shot to-morrow at nine."

And Lyman answered: "Shoot and be d——d."[63]

When some among the Saints, in an unthinking moment, betrayed the Prophet's love by accusing him of cowardice, he set his face toward Carthage Jail and martyrdom, declaring, "If my life is of no value to my friends it is of none to myself."[64] But even in this decision there were those who pledged to accompany him. "As you make your bed, I will lie with you," Orrin Porter Rockwell promptly asserted.[65] Later, as Joseph and his brother were about to enter the cell of the jail, the Prophet turned to Dr. Willard Richards and said, "If we go into the cell, will you go in with us?" Without hesitation the answer came: "Brother Joseph, you did not ask me to cross the river with you—you

---

[63]Evans, op. cit., pp. 136-137.
[64]History of the Church, VI, p. 549.
[65]Ibid. Said the Prophet: "I discover hundreds and thousands of my brethren ready to sacrifice their lives for me."—Ibid., p. 516.

did not ask me to come to Carthage—you did not ask me to come to jail with you—and do you think I would forsake you now? But I will tell you what I will do; If you are condemned to be hung for treason, I will be hung in your stead, and you shall go free." Joseph exclaimed, "You cannot." And the doctor replied, "I will."[66]

The responsibility to rebuke unrighteousness was associated with Joseph Smith's formula for rule and government by love. Many times he rebuked false traditions and practices. Other times an erring one would feel the lash of rebuke, used in an effort to reclaim him from his evil ways. The Prophet also found it necessary at times to rebuke the wilfully wicked and perverse. But whatever the role, he was a master at the art. He possessed a keen ability to draw the line between truth and error, sincerity and hypocrisy; and against the latter he spoke out without fear. "The Saints need not think because I am familiar with them and am playful and cheerful, that I am ignorant of what is going on," he once declared. "Iniquity of any kind cannot be sustained in the Church, and it will not fare well where I am; for I am determined while I do lead the Church, to lead it right."[67] Said George Q. Cannon:

> He was a great hater of sham. He disliked long-faced hypocrisy, and numerous stories are told of his peculiar manner of rebuking it. He knew that much that people call sin is not sin, and he did many things to break down superstition. He would wrestle, play ball, and enjoy himself in physical exercises, and he knew that he was not committing sin to do so. The religion of heaven is not to make men sorrowful, to curtail their enjoyment and to make them groan and sigh and wear long faces, but to make them happy. This

---

[66]*Ibid.*, VI, p. 616.
[67]*Ibid.*, V, p. 411.

Joseph desired to teach the people, but in doing so,
he, like our Savior, when he was on the earth, was
a stumbling block to bigots and hypocrites. They
could not understand him; he shocked their preju-
dices and traditions.[68]

Wilford Woodruff reported that once two ministers
had visited Joseph Smith at his home one Sunday after-
noon. As they concluded their visit and stepped outside,
Joseph drew a line on the ground with the heel of his shoe,
toed the mark, and made a jump. After marking the place
where he landed, he addressed them with the challenge,
"Which one of you can beat that?" The pious ministers
were shocked at such conduct on the Sabbath day; and that
is what the Prophet expected. He could easily discern
their pharisaical natures and knew that they came only to
look for faults. So he gave them an opportunity to criti-
cize by openly disdaining their narrow views and notions.[69]

In other ways the Prophet took note of error and followed his own course to rebuke and correct it. He once
reproved the brethren for "giving way to too much excitement and warmth in debate."[70] On another occasion he had
requested a brother to ask the blessing on the food he and
others were about to partake. The good man, having been
an exhorter in another faith before accepting Mormonism,
went at his duty with all his soul. He commenced to call
upon the great and mighty God who sat upon the top of a
topless throne, to look down and bless the food and asked
many other blessings to rest upon the Prophet. When he
concluded, Joseph said, "Brother Joshua, don't let me ever
hear you ask another such blessing." The good man was
somewhat taken back, but before they partook of the meal
the Prophet stated his reasons for making this correction

[68]*The Historical Record, op. cit.,* p. 489.
[69]Related in *Stories about Joseph Smith the Prophet,* pp. 17-18.
[70]*Juvenile Instructor,* XXVII, p. 399.

and showed how inconsistent such practices were when one understood the true concept of God.[71]

At times the Prophet found it necessary to use more than the spoken word in rebuking improprieties among others. The frontier and semi-frontier conditions of the day often fostered a roughness and rowdiness among men that, to be properly controlled, had to be dealt with on its own level. Benjamin F. Johnson later reported, "In the early days at Kirtland, and elsewhere, one or another of his associates were more than once, for their impudence, helped from the congregation by his foot, and at one time at a meeting at Kirtland, for insolence to him, he soundly thrashed his brother William who boasted himself an invincible."[72]

On another occasion Joseph wrote in his *Journal,* "Josiah Butterfield came to my house and insulted me so outrageously that I kicked him out of the house, across the yard, and into the street."[73]

The Missouri days were trying ones for the Saints. Many prominent men who had shared the Prophet's confidence became disaffected and proved to be his bitterest enemies. Some had previously witnessed great spiritual manifestations, but later they fell into transgression, partook of the spirit of hatred that was manifested against the Saints, and were largely responsible for shedding innocent blood. In the Prophet's view, they had seriously transgressed against the powers of God and were approaching a condition where there could be "no more sacrifice for sin." In a letter, written in Liberty Jail, December 16, 1838, he struck out against these dissenters with blunt satire, exclaiming:

---

[71]Reported by Daniel D. Tyler, *Juvenile Instructor,* XXVII, p. 129.
[72]Johnson to Gibbs, p. 4.
[73]*History of the Church,* V, p. 316.

Look at the dissenters. . . . Look at Mr.
Hinkle—a wolf in sheep's clothing. Look at his
brother John Corrill. Look at the beloved brother
Reed Peck, who aided him in leading us, as the
Savior was led, into the camp of His enemies, as
a lamb prepared for the slaughter, as a sheep
dumb before his shearers; so we opened not our
mouths.

But these men, like Balaam, being greedy for
reward, sold us into the hands of those who loved
them, for the world loves his own. I would
remember William E. McLellin, who comes up to
us as one of Job's comforters. God suffered such
kind of beings to afflict Job—but it never entered
into their hearts that Job would get out of it all.
This poor man who professes to be much of a
prophet, has no other dumb ass to ride but David
Whitmer [McLellin claimed that the Prophet had
fallen and sought to re-organize the Church with
David Whitmer as President], to forbid his mad-
ness when he goes up to curse Israel; and this ass
not being of the same kind as Balaam's, therefore,
the angel notwithstanding appeared unto him,
yet he could not penetrate his understanding sufficiently, but that he brays out cursings instead of
blessings. Poor ass! Whoever lives to see it,
will see him and his rider perish like those who
perished in the gainsaying of Korah, or after the
same condemnation. . . .

Such characters God hates; we cannot love
them. The world hates them, and we sometimes
think that the devil ought to be ashamed of
them. . . .

In fine, we have waded through an ocean of
tribulation and mean abuse, practiced upon us by
the ill bred and the ignorant, such as Hinkle,
Corrill, Phelps, Avard, Reed Peck, Cleminson,
and various others, who are so very ignorant that
they cannot appear respectable in any decent and

civilized society, and whose eyes are full
of adultery, and cannot cease from sin. Such
characters as McLellin, John Whitmer, David
Whitmer, Oliver Cowdery, and Martin Harris,
are too mean to mention; and we had liked to have
forgotten them. Marsh and "another," whose
hearts are full of corruption, whose cloak of hypocrisy was not sufficient to shield them or to hold
them up in the hour of trouble, who after having
escaped the pollutions of the world through the
knowledge of their Lord and Savior Jesus Christ,
became again entangled and overcome—their latter end is worse than the first.[74]

William W. Phelps was one of those referred to by
the Prophet. He not only betrayed Joseph's trust but also
testified against him and the Saints, justifying the course
of their enemies in many things. Later he sought to in-
volve himself in the settlement of certain of the Church's
financial matters. But Joseph Smith wrote him a sharp
note informing him that the Saints had "already experienced much over-officiousness" at his hands and requested
that he "avoid all interference in our business or affairs
from this time henceforth and forever."[75] But when Phelps
later came to himself and recognized the error of his ways,
he expressed a desire "to make any sacrifice" to procure the
forgiveness and friendship of the Prophet, "life not excepted." And in the greatness of the Prophet's soul, after
alluding to the tribulations he and others had passed through
largely as a result of the actions of false brethren, Joseph
wrote:

However, the cup has been drunk, the will of
our Father has been done, and we are yet alive,
for which we thank the Lord. And having been

---

[74]*Ibid.,* III, pp. 228, 230, 232.
[75]See *ibid.,* pp. 3, 7, 56, 358, 359, 360.

delivered from the hands of wicked men by the
mercy of our God, we say it is your privilege to be
delivered from the powers of the adversary, be
brought into the liberty of God's dear children,
and again take your stand among the Saints of
the Most High.[76]

The limitations placed upon the Prophet as a prisoner
in Missouri did not prevent him from rebuking unrighteousness, whether it was manifested by false brethren or by
corrupt guards.   On one occasion a leader among their
captors made a rather hard insinuation against some of the
brethren.   Said Alexander McRae, who was present:

This touched Joseph's feelings, and he retorted a good deal in the same way, only with such
power that the earth seemed to tremble under his
feet, and said, "Your heart is as black as your
whiskers," which were as black as any crow.   He
seemed to quake under it and left the room.[77]

In concluding his narration, McRae said of the Prophet, "He always took up for the brethren, when their characters were assailed, sooner than for himself, no matter
how unpopular it was to speak in their favor."[78]

The classic example of the Prophet's power to rebuke
is related by Parley P. Pratt.   While the brethren were
confined as prisoners in a vacant house at Richmond, Missouri, they lay together in chains under heavy guard, while
their tormentors recounted and boasted of their deeds of
rapine, robbery, and murder which they had committed
among the Mormons.   Said Pratt:

They even boasted of defiling by force, wives,
daughters and virgins, and of shooting or lashing

---

[76]*Ibid.,* IV, pp. 142-143, 162-163.
[77]*Ibid.,* III, p. 259.
[78]*Idem.*

out the brains of men, women and children. I had
listened until I became so disgusted, shocked, hor-
rified, and so filled with the spirit of indignant justice that I could scarcely refrain from rising upon
my feet and rebuking the guards; but had said
nothing to Joseph, or anyone else, although I lay
next to him and knew he was awake. On a sudden
he rose to his feet and spoke in the voice of thun-
der, or as a roaring lion, uttering, as nearly as I
can recollect, the following words:

"Silence, ye fiends of the eternal pit! In the
name of Jesus Christ I rebuke you, and command
you to be still; I will not live another minute and
hear such language. Cease such talk, or you or I
die this instant!"

He ceased to speak. He stood erect, in terrible majesty. Chained, and without a weapon;
calm, unruffled, and dignified as an angel, he
looked upon the quailing guards, whose weapons
were lowered, or dropped to the ground; whose
knees smote together, and who, shrinking into a
corner or crouching at his feet, begged his pardon,
and remained quiet till a change of guards."[79]

While recalling this incident, Parley P. Pratt later
wrote, "I have seen the ministers of justice, clothed in
magisterial robes, and criminals arraigned before them,
while life was suspended on a breath, in the courts of England; I have witnessed a congress in solemn session, to give
laws to a nation; I have tried to conceive of kings, of royal
courts, of thrones and crowns; of emperors assembled to
decide the fate of kingdoms; but dignity and majesty have
I seen but once, as it stood in chains, at midnight, in a
dungeon, in an obscure village in Missouri."[80]

---

[79]*Autobiography of Parley P. Pratt*, pp. 228-230.
[80]*Idem.*

III.

Education and Early Experiences

Joseph Smith had little opportunity to acquire a formal education, for the Smith family's financial circumstances during his youth made it almost impossible. Furthermore, it is generally agreed by authorities on America's social and cultural history during the first quarter of the nineteenth century that existing educational facilities, particularly on the common-school level, were in a deplorable condition. In New York the planned state-wide program of education was allowed to lag; and by 1830 there was still no general provision for universal education. Even in New England the state of affairs was shocking, particularly in the rural or district schools. There, New England's once praised common schools were grossly neglected and offered possible even less opportunity for education than they had done a century earlier.[1]

Noah Webster's "speller" and Emerson's history text were not yet available when Joseph Smith went to school. S. G. Goodrich, writing under the name of "Peter Parley," waited until 1827 to popularize geography by presenting this discipline in the form of the supposed travels of a boy visiting various countries of the world. And Rev. C. A. Goodrich's works in American history came some years after Joseph Smith's opportunity for formal education. The country had not yet awakened to the need of education for

---

[1]See Frederick Jackson Turner, *The United States, 1830-1850* (New York, 1935), p. 17; Merle Curti, *The Growth of American Thought* (New York and London, 1943), pp. 213-215; Carl Russell Fish, *The Rise of the Common Man* (New York, 1929), pp. 201-202; Alice Felt Tyler, *Freedom's Ferment* (Minneapolis, 1944), pp. 235-236.

The Prophet Joseph Smith from an early newspaper illustration.

the masses. It was after 1830 that Horace Mann and his associates began slowly to elevate the level of public schools in New England and adjacent areas.[2]

For the above reasons Joseph Smith had little opportunity to acquire more than the meager essentials of formal learning. John Taylor, Wilford Woodruff, and Charles C. Rich referred to him as an "illiterate and unlearned boy."[3] His cousin, George A. Smith, spoke of him as "a ploughboy, . . . one who cultivated the earth, and had scarcely education enough to read his Bible."[4] And Orson Pratt stated that he "was scarcely in possession of an ordinary common school education."[5] Again, Pratt wrote:

> His advantages for acquiring scientific knowledge were exceedingly small, being limited to a slight acquaintance with two or three of the common branches of learning. He could read without much difficulty, and write a very imperfect hand; and had a very limited understanding of the elementary rules of arithmetic. These were his highest and only attainments; while the rest of those branches, so universally taught in the common schools throughout the United States, were entirely unknown to him.[6]

Joseph Smith referred at times to his deficiencies in formal education. Said he, "I am a rough stone. The sound of the hammer and chisel was never heard on me until the Lord took me in hand. I desire the learning of heaven alone."[7] Again, he spoke of his experiences in the School of Hard Knocks:

---

[2]See Robert E. Regiel, *Young America 1830-1840* (Norman, Oklahoma, 1949), pp. 237-239; Tyler, *op. cit.*, p. 238.

[3]*J. D.*, XVIII, pp. 118, 210; XIX, p. 28.

[4]*J. D.*, VII, p. 111.

[5]*J. D.*, XII, p. 357. On another occasion Pratt referred to him as "but an ignorant farmer's boy, scarcely having the first rudiments of education."—*J. D.*, XVIII, p. 157. See also XVII, pp. 283-284.

[6]Orson Pratt, *Remarkable Visions* (Liverpool, England, 1848), p. 1.

[7]*History of the Church*, V, p. 423.

I am like a huge, rough stone rolling down from a high mountain; and the only polishing I get is when some corner gets rubbed off by coming in contact with something else, striking with accelerated force against religious bigotry, priest-craft, lawyer-craft, doctor-craft, lying editors, suborned judges and jurors, and the authority of perjured executives, backed by mobs, blasphemers, licentious and corrupt men and women—all hell knocking off a corner here and a corner there. Thus I will become a smooth and polished shaft in the quiver of the Almighty, who will give me dominion over all and every one of them, when their refuge of lies shall fail, and their hiding place shall be destroyed, while these smooth-polished stones with which I come in contact become marred.[8]

But while the Prophet lacked formal education he had an unquenchable thirst for truth, and he absorbed ideas like a sponge. He possessed that superior intelligence that enables one to go to the heart of things, discern that which is relevant, and see it in its true relationship to related facts and circumstances. In his later studies of Hebrew and Greek he outstripped his fellows, including Sidney Rigdon and Orson Pratt. When asked how the Prophet had progressed in his study of English grammar, one of his teachers replied, "Joseph was the calf that sucked three cows. He acquired knowledge very rapidly."[9]

With his power to assimilate truth, Joseph Smith possessed great natural ability. An acquaintance observed that he was "a man of great penetration."[10] Said another, "I considered him an uncommon man in ability."[11] While Zion's Camp was journeying toward Missouri in June,

[8]*Ibid.*, p. 401.
[9]See Ray B. West, Jr., *Kingdom of the Saints* (New York, 1957), p. 61.
[10]Statement by Bathsheba W. Smith, *Juvenile Instructor*, XXVII, p. 344.
[11]Statement by Edson Barney, *ibid.*, p. 256 .

1834, the brethren held a Sunday service, which was attended by two or three hundred people from the surrounding area. The Prophet, posing as Squire Cook, took the stand professing to be a liberal freethinker. Said George A. Smith, "He spoke to the people very freely about one hour on his particular views; his manner and style were very unassuming and affable, and he was listened to with great attention; and those present remarked that he was one of the greatest reasoners they ever heard."[12]

Aside from his natural capacities, it was Joseph's superior insight into spiritual truth that baffled the sectarians of Palmyra. Some years after the Smiths had moved from that area, E. L. and William H. Kelley, who resided in Michigan, visited Palmyra and interviewed several people who were formerly acquainted with the Prophet.

"Smith was always ready to exchange views with the best men they had," remarked one acquaintance.

"Why didn't they like Smith?" the Kelleys inquired.

"To tell the truth," came the significant reply, "there was something about him they could not understand; someway he knew more than they did, and it made them mad."[13]

In a letter to E. D. Howe, written from Canadaigua, New York, January 15, 1831, William W. Phelps gave a report that corroborated the above statement. He said, after asserting that he was "acquainted with a number of the persons concerned in the publication" of the Book of Mormon, "Joseph Smith is a person of very limited abilities in common learning, but his knowledge of divine things, since the appearance of his book, has astonished many."[14]

---

[12]George A. Smith's *Journal*, June 1, 1834. For security reasons the brethren kept their identity unknown.
[13]*The Saints Herald*, Plano, Illinois, XI (June 1, 1881), p. 167.
[14]*Journal History*, January 15, 1831. Phelps was not then a member of the Church.

The Prophet's insight into spiritual truth drew others to him and transformed them into zealous disciples. To Brigham Young the contemporary sectarians "were as blind as Egyptian darkness," without correct information "about heaven, hell, God, angels, or devils." But, said he, "When I saw Joseph Smith, he took heaven, figuratively speaking, and brought it down to earth; and he took the earth, brought it up, and opened up, in plainness and simplicity, the things of God; and that is the beauty of his mission."[15] Orson Spencer also wrote, "At his touch the ancient prophets spring into life, and the beauty and power of their revelations are made to commend themselves with thrilling interest to all that hear."[16] Said the sober-minded, thoughtful Daniel H. Wells of his observations:

> Though I did not at first believe that he was inspired or that he was more than a man of great natural ability, I soon learned that he knew more about religion and the things of God and eternity than any man I had ever heard talk. . . . It seemed to me that he advanced principles that neither he nor any other man could have obtained except from the source of all wisdom—the Lord himself. I soon discovered that he was not what the world termed a well-read or an educated man; then where could he have got this knowledge and understanding, that so far surpassed all I had ever witnessed, unless it had come from Heaven?[17]

Others bore a similar testimony of the intelligence, power, and inspiration of Joseph's teachings. Parley P. Pratt reported his travels with the Prophet, "As we journeyed day after day, and generally lodged together, we had much sweet communion concerning the things of God and the mysteries of His kingdom, and I received many

---

[15]*J. D.,* V, p. 332.
[16]Spencer, *op. cit.,* p. 27.
[17]*J. D.,* XII, p. 72.

admonitions and instructions which I shall never forget."[18] Erastus Snow spoke of his association with the Prophet during the winter and spring of 1844, when the higher ordinances of the gospel and the more complete vision of the kingdom of God, which includes a political order as well as a Church, were taught to the brethren. Though he had been in the Church for some time and had been a keen student of spiritual and secular truth for many years, he wrote in his *Journal*: "The precious instructions which I received in the councils of the Church during that winter and spring were indeed more than all I had learned before in my life."[19] Out of his background of learning and refinement John Taylor could also speak of the Prophet, stating, "He was ignorant of letters as the world has it, but the most profoundly learned and intelligent man in after life that I have ever met in my life, and I have traveled hundreds of thousands of miles, been on different continents, and mingled among all classes and creeds of people, yet I have never met a man so intelligent as Joseph Smith."[20] Said Brigham Young of his desire to drink from the Prophet's fountain of truth:

> In my experience I never did let an opportunity pass of getting with the Prophet Joseph and of hearing him speak in public or in private, so that I might draw understanding from the fountain from which he spoke, that I might have it and bring it forth when it was needed. . . .
>
> In the days of the Prophet Joseph, such moments were more precious to me than all the wealth

---

[18]*Autobiography of Parley Parker Pratt* (Salt Lake City, 1938), p. 110. In his first meeting with Joseph Smith, Pratt reported listening to an address by the Prophet, "filled with intelligence and wisdom."—*Journal History*, September, 1830.

[19]Erastus Snow's *Journal*, immediately preceding the entry for April 6, 1844. Church Historian's Office, Salt Lake City, Utah. For a treatment of the Prophet's concept of the kingdom of God, see Hyrum L. Andrus, *Joseph Smith and World Government*, Salt Lake City, 1958.

[20]*J. D.*, XXI, p. 163.

of the world. No matter how great my poverty—
if I had to borrow meal to feed my wife and
children, I never let an opportunity pass of learning what the Prophet had to impart. This is the
secret of success of your humble servant.[21]

The principal source of the Prophet's appeal was the
intelligence and power which he possessed in spiritual
things. Even as a lad of fourteen he displayed power by
faith to penetrate the spiritual veil and stand in the presence
of God. The great manifestations which he experienced
came not without intense effort on his part. Before he
communed with Moroni that evening in September, 1823,
he retired to his room in what his mother later described as
a "serious and contemplative state of mind."[22] There, with
unwavering faith, he sought the favor of God, for, said he,
"I had full confidence in obtaining a divine manifestation,
as I previously had done."[23] While absorbed in the con-
centration of faith his mind was "settled upon a determined
basis not to be decoyed or driven from its purpose," Oliver
Cowdery later wrote of this incident. "In this situation
hours passed unnumbered—how many or how few I know
not, neither is he able to inform me; but supposes it must
have been eleven or twelve and perhaps later, as the noise
and bustle of the family, in retiring, had long since ceased."[24]

Here was a young man so intent upon concentrating
his energies and applying his desires toward communion
with God that he lost all sense of time. He had but one
ambition, and that was to come into the presence of his
Maker.

In a theological school held in Kirtland during the
winter of 1834-5, Heber C. Kimball related a story of simple

---

[21]*J. D.*, XII, pp. 269-270.
[22]Smith, *op. cit.*, p. 77.
[23]*History of the Church*, I, p. 11.
[24]*Messenger and Advocate*, February, 1835.

faith that touched a responsive cord in the Prophet's heart and revealed the quality of faith which he possessed. Kimball's little daughter had broken a saucer and for the act was promised a whipping, to be administered by her mother when she returned from a visit on which she was just starting. While her mother was away, the girl went out under an apple tree and prayed that her mother's heart might be softened so that the promised punishment might not be administered. Mrs. Kimball was very careful to fulfill her promises to her children, but upon returning she had no disposition to chastise her child. Later the child told her mother that she had prayed to God that she might not receive the whipping. "Joseph wept like a child on hearing this simple narrative and its application," Kimball reported.[25]

In the Prophet's reaction may be found a key to his nature. He, too, knew the power of childlike faith. Hence the narration of that simple incident deeply touched him. At another time he sat down to eat a scanty meal of corn bread, and prayed, "Lord, we thank Thee for this johnny cake, and ask Thee to send us something better. Amen." Before the bread had been eaten, a man came to the door and asked if Joseph were home, and upon being informed that he was, said, "I have brought you some flour and a ham." After thanking the man and blessing him for the gift, the Prophet turned to his wife and said, "I knew the Lord would answer my prayer."[26] On another occasion when the Prophet's enemies were threatening him with violence, he was told that quite a number of little children were then gathered together, praying for his safety. To this he commented, "Then I need have no fear; I am safe."[27]

Newel Knight wrote of the second conference of the

[25]*Journal History*, December 22, 1834.
[26]*Juvenile Instructor*, XXVII, p. 172.
[27]*Young Woman's Journal*, XVI, p. 550.

Church, held September 26, 1830, that the powers of God were markedly manifested through the Prophet's faith. Shortly before the conference, Hiram Page had obtained a certain stone through which he professed to receive revelations concerning church government, the location of the New Jerusalem, etc. "He had quite a roll of papers full of these revelations, and many in the Church were led astray by them," Knight reported. "Even Oliver Cowdery and the Whitmer family had given heed to them, although they were in contradiction to the New Testament and the revelations of these last days." When Knight arrived on the scene of the conference, he found Joseph in great distress of mind; he "was perplexed and scarcely knew how to meet this new exigency." As may be expected, Joseph turned to God in prayer and supplication. A brief but meaningful insight into the Prophet's character was given when Knight reported, "That night I occupied the same room that he did and the greater part of the night was spent in prayer and supplication."[28]

The following day a revelation was given through the Prophet, by which those in error were reproved and corrected, and peace was restored within the Church. Wrote Newel Knight of that conference:

> During this time we had much of the power of God manifested among us and it was wonderful to witness the wisdom that Joseph displayed on this occasion, for truly God gave unto him great wisdom and power, and it seems to me, even now, that none who saw him administer righteousness under such trying circumstances, could doubt that the Lord was with him, as he acted—not with the wisdom of man, but with the wisdom of God. The Holy Ghost came upon us and filled our hearts with unspeakable joy.[29]

---

[28]*Journal History*, September 26, 1830.
[29]*Idem.*

Later as Joseph was endeavoring to build the Kirtland Temple, several of the brethren rebelled against him, including his brother William. Daniel Tyler reported attending a meeting that the Prophet called to consider the matter. Upon entering the place of the meeting and looking at Joseph, said Tyler,

> I perceived sadness in his countenance and tears trickling down his cheeks. . . . A few moments later a hymn was sung and he opened the meeting by prayer. Instead, however, of facing the audience, he turned his back and bowed upon his knees, facing the wall . . . to hide his sorrow and tears.
>
> I had heard men and women pray—especially the former—from the most ignorant, both as to letters and intellect, to the most learned and eloquent, but never until then had I heard a man address his Maker as though He was present listening as a kind father would listen to the sorrows of a dutiful child. Joseph was at that time unlearned, but that prayer, which was to a considerable extent in behalf of those who accused him of having gone astray and fallen into sin, that the Lord would forgive them and open their eyes that they might see aright—that prayer, I say, to my humble mind, partook of the learning and eloquence of heaven. There was no ostentation, no raising of the voice as by enthusiasm, but a plain conversational tone, as a man would address a present friend. It appeared to me as though, in case the veil were taken away, I could see the Lord standing facing His humblest of all servants I had ever seen. Whether this was really the case I cannot say; but one thing I can say, it was the crowning . . . of all the prayers I ever heard.[30]

In the early months of 1837, when apostasy was spread-

---

[30]*Juvenile Instructor*, XXVII, p. 129.

ing throughout the Church, the Prophet's spiritual strength again aided him to cope with dissension among the brethren. He had been away from Kirtland for a short period and returned to find that many were disaffected. Said Wilford Woodruff, "Though he had not been away half as long as Moses was in the Mount, yet many were against him as the Israelites were against Moses; but when he arose in the power of God in the midst of them, they were put to silence; for the murmurers saw that he stood in the power of a Prophet of the Lord God."[31]

Reports by others corroborate the above accounts of the spiritual powers associated with the Prophet's administrations. In his *Journal*, Jared Carter gave the following report of the conference held June 3, 1831:

On this occasion Brother Joseph, notwithstanding he was not naturally a talented speaker, was filled with the power of the Holy Ghost, and spoke as I never heard man speak for God before. Surely the Holy Ghost spoke through him and marvelous, indeed, was the display of the power of the Spirit among the Elders present.[32]

Said Wilford Woodruff of a conference held in April, 1837:

The Prophet Joseph then arose and addressed the congregation for the space of three hours, clothed with the power, spirit and image of God. He presented many things of vast importance to the Elders of Israel. O! that the record could be written as with an iron pen of the light, principles and virtue that came forth out of the mouth and heart of the Prophet Joseph whose soul like Enoch's seems wide as eternity. That day showed

---

[31]*Journal History*, February 19, 1837.
[32]*Ibid.*, June 3, 1831. In his *Journal*, Newel Knight reported that "the power of the Lord was displayed in our midst."—*Ibid.*

strikingly that he is in very deed a Prophet of God raised up for the deliverance of Israel.[33]

Again, from the report of Wilford Woodruff of a later meeting:

> Joseph then arose and like the lion of the Tribe of Judah poured out his soul in the midst of the congregation of Saints. While listening I thought, "Who can find language to write his words and teachings as with an iron pen in a rock, that they might stand for future generations to look upon!" He seemed a fountain of knowledge from whose mouth streams of eternal wisdom flowed; and as he stood before the people he showed that the authority of God was upon him.[34]

While Joseph Smith was denied the privilege of a formal education in his youth, his natural endowments and simple but superior faith opened unto him a world of truth and power that commanded for him a hearing among men. Above all, his faith was his most valuable credential as a Prophet of God.

Joseph Smith's insight into spiritual truth came largely as a by-product of the things he saw in vision. In the spring of 1820, when he was a lad of fourteen, there was a religious awakening in certain parts of the country, particularly in the state of New York; and in common with others, young Joseph was stimulated to inquire into religious topics. In central-western New York and adjacent areas, a great number of people became sympathetic toward the established churches, but at first only few were actually enrolled as members. Quite naturally the goal was to bring those who were interested into actual membership. Consequently, when a revival gained momentum in a given place,

---

[33]*Ibid.*, April 6, 1837.
[34]*Ibid.*, April 9, 1837.

preachers from outside areas would flock into the agitated neighborhood, for the desire of each denomination was to build up its membership from the available interested persons. To stimulate religious interest generally, the several ministers would co-operate in the beginning stages of the revival season, for the interests of all were served by their aiding in the development of enthusiasm. But when the question of which church to join was considered, the struggle for converts followed. Joseph Smith later wrote of these circumstances, stating:

Some time in the second year after our removal to Manchester, there was in the place where we lived an unusual excitement, on the subject of religion. It commenced with the Methodists, but soon became general among all the sects in that region of country. Indeed, the whole district of country seemed affected by it, and great multitudes united themselves to the different religious parties, which created no small stir and division amongst the people, some crying, "Lo here!" and others, "Lo there!" Some were contending for the Methodist faith, some for the Presbyterian, and some for the Baptist. For, notwithstanding the great love which the converts to these different faiths expressed at the time of their conversion, and the great zeal manifested by the respective clergy, who were active in getting up and promoting this extraordinary scene of religious feeling, in order to have everyone converted, as they were pleased to call it, let them join what sect they pleased; yet when the converts began to file off, some to one party and some to another, it was seen that the seemingly good feelings of both the priests and the converts were more pretended than real; for a scene of great confusion and bad feeling ensued— priest contending against priest, and convert against convert; so that all their good feelings one for another, if they ever had any, were entirely

lost in a strife of words and a contest about opin-
ions.[35]

The Methodists held their annual meeting of the Genesee Conference July 1-8, 1819 at Vienna (now Phelps),
about ten miles from where the Smiths lived. Though
characterized by contention, Abner Chase (a minister at
the conference) states that it "was followed by a glorious
revival." During the winter of 1819-20, revivals also occurred in other nearby towns.[36]

The prevailing contention caused Joseph to inquire,
"Who of all these parties are right?" While pondering the
issue, he read James, chapter one, verse five: "If any of
you lack wisdom, let him ask of God, that giveth to all
men liberally, and upbraideth not; and it shall be given
him."[37] He said:

Never did any passage of scripture come with
more power to the heart of man than this did at
this time to mine. It seemed to enter with great
force into every feeling of my heart. I reflected
on it again and again, knowing that if any person
needed wisdom from God, I did; for how to act I
did not know, and unless I could get more wisdom
than I then had, I would never know; for the
teachers of religion of the different sects understood the same passages of scripture so differently
as to destroy all confidence in settling the question
by an appeal to the Bible. At length I came to the
conclusion that I must either remain in darkness
and confusion, or else I must do as James directs,

[36]See F. W. Conable, *History of the Genesee Annual Conference of the
Methodist Episcopal Church* (New York, 1885), pp. 142, 158-159, 166, 175;
James H. Hotchkin, *A History of the Purchase and Settlement of Western New
York and the Rise, Progress, and Present State of the Presbyterian Church in
that Section* (New York, 1848), pp. 135, 379; "Records of the Presbytery of
Geneva," pp. 36-38; "Records of the Synod of Geneva," p. 220.
[37]*History of the Church*, I, pp. 3-4.

that is, ask of God. I at length came to the deter-
mination to "ask of God," concluding that if he
gave wisdom to them that lacked wisdom, and
would give liberally, and not upbraid, I might ven-
ture.[38]

On a beautiful, clear day, early in the spring of 1820,
Joseph retired to pray in a wooded area near his home. He
had scarcely commenced when he was "seized upon by some
power" which entirely overcame him and had such influence over him as to bind his tongue so that he could not
speak. As thick darkness gathered around him, he exerted
all his strength to call upon God to deliver him from the
power of his unseen enemy.[39]

At that moment he saw a brilliant light at a considerable distance in the heavens above. When it appeared,
the enemy fled. Joseph continued to pray as the light
gradually descended towards him, "and as it drew near,
it increased in brightness and magnitude, so that by the
time that it reached the tops of the trees, the whole wilderness, for some distance around, was illuminated in a most
glorious and brilliant manner." He saw that it did not
consume the boughs of the trees and he was encouraged
with the hopes of being able to endure its presence. As the
light rested upon him, "it produced a peculiar sensation
throughout his whole system; and immediately, his mind
was caught away from the natural objects with which he
was surrounded, and he was enwrapped in a heavenly
vision."[40]   Said the Prophet later:

When the light rested upon me I saw two
Personages, whose brightness and glory defy all

---

[38]*History of the Church,* I, p. 4.
[39]*Ibid.,* p. 5.
[40]Orson Pratt, *Remarkable Visions,* p. 2. This statement by Pratt is consistent
with that given by the Prophet, but in more detail. It is noteworthy that each time
Pratt related the First Vision he added these particulars. See J. D., XII, pp. 354-
356; XIV, p. 141; XV, p. 181; XVII, p. 279; XXII, p. 29,

description, standing above me in the air. One of them spake unto me, calling me by name and said, pointing to the other—*This is My Beloved Son. Hear Him!*[41]

When Joseph left the grove that spring morning, he possessed the essential spiritual truths upon which to launch the new dispensation of the gospel. The first person to whom he related his vision, outside of the Smith family, was a minister who was active in the revival. Joseph said: "He treated my communication not only lightly, but with great contempt, saying it was all of the devil, that there were no such things as visions or revelations in these days; that all such things had ceased with the apostles.[42] Others were later told of the incident. In the fall of 1824, Joseph Smith, Sr., and the Prophet's brother Hyrum were employed to work for Martin Harris. "On the occasion Mr. Harris showed an unusual interest in Joseph's vision in the Grove, stating that he was much interested in it." Because of his sincere interest, the Prophet's father "confided in him and explained more of the particulars concerning Joseph's experiences"[43] Thereafter the story of the Prophet's First Vision became common knowledge to those acquainted with Mormonism. On February 14, 1831, the *Palmyra*

---

[41]*History of the Church*, I, p. 5.

[42]*Ibid.*, pp. 6-7.

[43]William Bean, *A. B. C. History of Palmyra and the Beginning of Mormonism* (Palmyra, 1938), p. 35. Evidently, the Prophet's parents continued relating the incidents relative to the rise of the Church. Wandle Mace made the following report:

Almost as soon as the Father and Mother of the Prophet Joseph Smith set their feet upon the hospitable shore of Illinois, I became acquainted with them. I frequently visited them and listened with intense interest as they related the history of the rise of the Church in every detail.

With tears they could not withhold, they narrated the story of the persecution of their boy Joseph, which commenced when he was about fourteen years old; or from the time the angel first visited him and informed him of the great things the Lord was about to bring to pass . . . and the glorious vision he beheld, as he saw the Father and the Son descend to earth, when the Father said to the youth, "Joseph," pointing to His companion, "This is my beloved Son, hear Him."—Mace, *op. cit.*, pp. 45-46. The writer has corrected certain marks of punctuation in this quote.

Reflector reported on the testimony of early missionaries, stating: "Smith (they affirmed) had seen God frequently and personally.[44] John P. Greene wrote from Upper Canada, in 1834, stating that he had given the people "the testimony of the *New* and *Everlasting Covenant*, as established in these last days: being confirmed by many infallible proofs, both human and divine—the Lord himself speaking from the heavens unto men who were now living"[45] About that time Oliver Cowdery was accosted by a man who immediately commenced a tirade against the Mormon Prophet. Said Cowdery, "He said that the Savior had not been seen since his ascension, and that any man contradicting this was a deceiver."[46]

The Prophet himself bore testimony of his vision in public as well as in private. Edward Stevenson said of his missionary activities in Pontiac, Michigan, and vicinity:

> In that same year, 1834, in the midst of many large congregations, the Prophet testified with great power concerning the visit of the Father and the Son, and the conversation he had with them. Never before did I feel such power as was manifested on these occasions.[47]

---

[44]The implication that the Prophet had seen God more than once before 1831 may stem from the fact that the voice of God was heard when the Three Witnesses beheld the plates, at the restoration of the Aaronic Priesthood, and at the time the Prophet was commanded to organize the Church. See *History of the Church,* I, pp. 54, 60; *Times and Seasons,* II, p. 201; *Doctrine and Covenants,* 128:21.

[45]*Messenger and Advocate,* I (October, 1834), pp. 7-8.

[46]*Ibid.,* p. 4. One of the charges made against the Saints in Jackson County, Mo., was that they claimed to "hold converse with God and his angels."—*Jefferson Republic,* Jefferson City, Mo., VII (August 17, 1833), p. 2. *The Missouri Intelligencer and Boon Lick Advertiser,* Columbus Mo., XVII, (April 13, 1833), p. 1, quoted an article by B. Pixley, in the *Christian Watchman,* dated Independence, Jackson Co., Mo., October 12, 1832, as stating: "The Mormons still prefer to talk with angels, visit the third heaven, and converse with Christ face to face."

[47]Edward Stevenson, *Reminiscenses of Joseph, the Prophet, and the Coming Forth of the Book of Mormon* (Salt Lake City, 1893), pp. 4-5. That the Prophet related his spiritual experiences at an early date is evident also from the following statement by William Farrington Cahoon, who wrote of his first meeting with Joseph Smith in 1831. Said Cahoon: "My impression, after hearing Joseph bear his testimony of what he had seen, was that he was a Prophet of the Most High God."—*Juvenile Instructor,* XXVII, p. 492.

As a youth of seventeen, Joseph began a further schooling to equip him for the work of establishing the foundations of this last dispensation; and from then until his death he continued to be taught from on high. Therein he received the most unique and thorough education in spiritual matters ever given to man, with the exception of that which the Son of God received while in mortality. Oliver Cowdery later said of the appearance of Moroni, in September, 1823:

> While continuing in prayer for a manifestation in some way that his sins were forgiven, endeavoring to exercise faith in the scriptures, on a sudden a light like that of day, only of a purer and far more glorious appearance and brightness, burst into the room. Indeed, to use his own description, the first sight was as though the house filled with consuming and unquenchable fire. This sudden appearance of a light so bright, as must naturally be expected, occasioned a shock or sensation, visible to the extremities of the body. It was, however, followed with a calmness and serenity of mind, and an overwhelming rapture of joy that surpassed understanding, and in a moment a personage stood before him.
>
> Notwithstanding the room was previously filled with light above the brightness of the sun, . . . yet there seemed to be an additional glory surrounding or accompanying this personage, which shone with an increased degree of brilliancy, of which he was in the midst; and though his countenance was as lightning, yet it was of a pleasing, innocent and glorious appearance, so much so, that every fear was banished from the heart, and nothing but calmness pervaded the soul.[48]

The heavenly messenger called Joseph by name and

---

[48]*Messenger and Advocate*, February, 1835.

introduced himself as one sent from the presence of God. The Prophet was informed that "there was a book deposited, written upon gold plates, giving an account of the former inhabitants of this continent, and the source from whence they sprang." This record also contained the "fulness of the everlasting Gospel," as revealed by Christ to those ancient inhabitants. With it were a Urim and Thummim and certain other valuable articles. The Prophet later wrote, "While he was conversing with me about the plates, the vision was opened to my mind that I could see the place where the plates were deposited, and that so clearly and distinctly that I knew the place again when I visited it."[49]

Repeatedly during his communions with Moroni this celestial means of instruction was employed. Oliver Cowdery later explained:

> When God manifests to his servants those things that are to come, or those which have been, he does it by unfolding them by the power of that Spirit which comprehends all things, always; and so much may be shown and made perfectly plain to the understanding in a short time, that the world, who are occupied all their life to learn a little, look at the relation of it, and are disposed to call it false. *You will understand then, by this, that while those glorious things were being rehearsed, the vision was also opened, so that our brother was permitted to see and understand much more fully and perfectly than I am able to communicate in writing.*[50]

To illustrate his point, Cowdery cited the visions given to Moses, to the brother of Jared, and to others, as examples of the way in which Joseph Smith was taught by

[49]*History of the Church*, I, pp. 11-13.
[50]*Messenger and Advocate*, I (April, 1835), p. 112. (Italics by the writer.)

Moroni.[51] While enveloped in the powers of God's Spirit, Moses beheld "the earth, yea, even all of it; and there was not a particle of it which he did not behold, discerning it by the Spirit of God." By the same means he also beheld "the inhabitants thereof, and there was not a soul which he beheld not."[52] By means of those same powers, God "showed unto the brother of Jared all the inhabitants of the earth which had been, and also all that would be; and he withheld them not from his sight, even unto the ends of the earth."[53] In this manner also was Joseph taught.

John Taylor referred to this divine means of instruction, as employed in teaching the Prophet, in a letter to a clergyman in England. After stating that he had "conversed with three who . . . have communion with angels," Taylor wrote, "One of these observed that it was easy for him to conceive of how the Lord could teach a man more in five minutes than volumes would contain."[54] Wrote the Prophet concerning the visitation of Moroni, in his noted "Wentworth Letter": "I was informed concerning the aboriginal inhabitants of this country *and shown who they were, and from whence they came;* a brief sketch of their origin, progress, civilization, laws, governments, of their righteousness and iniquity, and the blessings of God being finally withdrawn from them as a people, was made known unto me."[55]

Joseph's mother gave corroborating evidence to support the Prophet's statement when she reported that after Moroni's initial visitations the Smith family often met together in the evening and gave the "most profound attention" to the third son, as he related the things he had heard and seen while in communion with the angel. Said she:

---

[51]*Idem.*
[52]Moses 1:27-28.
[53]Ether 3:25.
[54]*Messenger and Advocate,* III (June, 1837), pp. 513-514.
[55]*History of the Church,* IV, p. 537. (Italics by the writer.)

During our evening conversations, Joseph would occasionally give us some of the most amusing recitals that could be imagined. He would describe the ancient inhabitants of this continent, their dress, mode of traveling, and the animals upon which they rode; their cities, their buildings, with every particular; their mode of warfare; and also their religious worship. This he would do with as much ease, seemingly, as if he had spent his whole life among them.[56]

Wandle Mace, who became acquainted with the Prophet's parents shortly after they were driven from Missouri, frequently visited them and heard them relate the incidents pertaining to the early rise of the Church. Of the period commencing immediately after Moroni's initial visitations, he reported that Mother Smith said:

During the day our sons would endeavor to get through their work as early as possible, and say, "Mother, have supper early so we can have a long evening to listen to Joseph." Sometimes Joseph would describe the appearance of the Nephites, their mode of dress and warfare, their implements of husbandry, etc., and many things he had seen in vision.[57]

The period between 1823 and 1827 were years of instruction and correction for Joseph Smith. Oliver Cowdery explained that without being "favored with a certain round of experiences" his mind might have been "turned from correct principles." But, "While young, untraditioned,

---

[56]Smith, op. cit., pp. 82-83. Concerning the Urim and Thummim, Lucy Mack Smith also said: "It was by this that the angel showed him many things which he saw in vision."—Ibid., p. 110.

[57]Mace, op. cit., pp. 46-47. Said George Q. Cannon: "Moroni, in the beginning, as you know, to prepare him [Joseph] for his mission, came and ministered and talked to him from time to time, and he had vision after vision in order that his mind might be fully saturated with knowledge of the things of God, and that he might comprehend the great and holy calling that God has bestowed upon him."—J. D., XXIII, p. 362.

and untaught in the systems of the world, he was in a situation to be led into the great work of God, and be qualified to perform it in due time."[58]

One of these instructive experiences occurred the day after his initial interview with Moroni, as he went to the Hill Cumorah to view the plates. He had been admonished that in obtaining the record he must have an eye single to the glory of God. But instead, his thoughts were largely upon the prospects of worldly wealth that the gold plates could bring to him and his family. But, said Cowdery,

On attempting to take possession of the record, a shock was produced upon his system, by an invisible power, which deprived him, in a measure of his natural strength. He desisted for an instant, and then made another attempt, but was more sensibly shocked than before. What was the occasion of this he knew not—there was a pure unsullied record, as has been described—he had heard of the powers of enchantment, and a thousand like stories, which held the hidden treasures of the earth, and supposed that physical exertion and personal strength was only necessary to enable him to yet obtain the object of his wish. He therefore made a third attempt with an increased exertion, when his strength failed him more than at either of the former times, and without premeditating he exclaimed, "Why can I not obtain this book?" "Because you have not kept the commandments of the Lord," answered a voice, within a seeming short distance. He looked and to his astonishment there stood the angel who had previously given him the directions concerning this matter. In an instant, all the former instructions, the great intelligence concerning Israel and the last days were brought to his mind; he thought of the time when his heart was fervently engaged

---

[58]*Messenger and Advocate*, October, 1835.

in prayer to the Lord, when his spirit was contrite,
and when this holy messenger from the skies unfolded the wonderful things connected with this
record, . . . but he had failed to remember the
great end for which they had been kept, and in
consequence could not have power to take them
into his possession and bear them away.[59]

This chastisement was followed by another great les-
son, in which divine powers were again used to instruct
the young Prophet. In remorse and humility he looked to
the Lord in prayer. And as he did,

> . . . the heavens were opened and the glory
> of the Lord shone around about and rested upon
> him. While thus he stood gazing and admiring,
> the angel said, "Look!" and as he thus spake he
> beheld the prince of darkness, surrounded by his
> innumerable train of associates. All this passed
> before him, and the heavenly messenger said,
> "All this is shown, the good and the evil, the holy
> and the impure, the glory of God, the power of
> darkness, that ye may know hereafter the two
> powers and never be influenced or overcome by
> that wicked one. Behold, whatever entices and
> leads to good and to do good, is of God, and
> whatever does not is of that wicked one . . . and
> you may learn from henceforth, that his ways are
> to destruction, but the way of holiness is peace and
> rest."[60]

Other great truths were taught to the Prophet on this
occasion, and many future events were unfolded to his
view. Said the angel:

> When they [the records] are interpreted, the
> Lord will give the Holy Priesthood to some, and

---

[59]*Idem.*
[60]*Idem.*

they shall begin to proclaim the gospel and bap-
tize by water, and after that they shall have power
to give the Holy Ghost by the laying on of their
hands. Then will persecution rage more and
more, for the iniquities of men shall be revealed,
and those who are not built upon the rock will
seek to overthrow this Church; but it will increase
the more opposed, and spread farther and farther,
increasing in knowledge till they shall be sanctified
and receive an inheritance where the glory of
God shall rest upon them; and when this takes
place, and all things are prepared, the ten tribes
of Israel will be revealed in the north country,
whither they have been for a long season; and
when this is fulfilled will be brought to pass that
saying of the prophet—"And the Redeemer shall
come to Zion, and unto them that turn from transgression in Jacob, saith the Lord."[61]

Along with other admonitions, Moroni gave Joseph
the promise that in due time God would again give him "a
commandment to come and take" the plates. Following
this interview, the youthful prophet "continued to receive
instructions concerning the coming forth of the fulness of
the gospel, from the mouth of a heavenly messenger, until
he was directed to visit again the place where the records
were deposited."[62] As he visited the sacred repository
again, in September, 1824, he went fully expecting to get
the plates at that time. He supposed that the only require-
ment necessary to obtain them was to "keep the requirements of God." This he felt he could do. Among those
requirements was a strict injunction not to lay the plates
down or put them out of his hands until he could deposit
them in a safe place. But as he took the plates and turned
away, he thought perhaps he should return and cover the
box, and also check to see if perchance he had left any-

---

[61]*Idem.*
[62]*Idem.*

thing therein.   After laying the plates down upon the
ground, he returned.   And as he turned again to pick up
the record, it was gone.   In a state of great alarm he commenced to pray, whereupon the angel appeared unto him
and chastised him for his neglect.   He was then permitted
again to raise the stone that covered the repository, and
therein he beheld the plates.   According to his mother's
account,

> He immediately reached forth his hand to
> take them, but instead of getting them as he antici-
> pated, he was hurled back upon the ground with
> great violence.   When he recovered, the angel
> was gone, and he arose and returned to the house,
> weeping for grief and disappointment.[63]

The Prophet's mother relates another incident that
indicates that the years between 1823 and 1827 were preparatory years, and that Joseph Smith learned much to
equip him for his later mission in life.   A few months before
the Prophet finally received the ancient records, his father
sent him on an errand to Manchester, a short distance from
the Smith home.   He was to be back before 6 p.m., but
it was sometime thereafter before he arrived.   As he entered the house, his father began questioning him as to
where he had been, whereupon Joseph said, "I have taken
the severest chastisement that I have ever had in my life."
When his father then begin to interrogate him as to who
had a right to find fault in him, the Prophet answered,

> "Stop, Father, stop, it was the angel of the
> Lord.   As I passed by the hill of Cumorah, where
> the plates are, the angel met me and said that I had
> not been engaged enough in the work of the Lord;
> that the time had come for the record to be brought

---

[63]Smith, op. cit., pp. 83-84.

forth; and that I must be up and doing and set myself about the things which God had commanded me to do. But, Father, give yourself no uneasiness concerning the reprimand which I have received, for I now know the course that I am to pursue, so all will be well."[64]

It was also made known unto Joseph at this interview "that he should make another effort to obtain the plates, on the twenty-second of the following September."[65] This time he was successful in obtaining the Nephite record. By then he had been sufficiently instructed and disciplined to the point where he could be entrusted with the care of the plates and the task of translating them for the benefit of mankind. The period between 1823 and 1827 was indeed an important time in Joseph Smith's life.

---

[64]*Ibid.*, pp. 99-101.
[65]*Ibid.*, p. 101.

IV.

Joseph Smith and the Ministry of Angels

Angels have a vital ministry to perform in the earth, in bringing about the purposes of God. Among other things, their mission is to reveal those truths and to supply that evidence to men upon which true faith in God can be built. In this capacity, they reveal themselves unto those of "strong faith and a firm mind in every form of godliness." Mormon said:

> And the office of their ministry is to call men unto repentance, and to fulfill and to do the work of the covenants of the Father, which he hath made unto the children of men, to prepare the way among the children of men, by declaring the word of Christ unto the chosen vessels of the Lord, that they may bear testimony of him.
>
> And by so doing, the Lord God prepareth the way that the residue of men may have faith in Christ, that the Holy Ghost may have place in their hearts, according to the power thereof; and after this manner bringeth to pass the Father, the covenants which he hath made unto the children of men.[1]

Salvation is made possible through the ministry of angels, first, by God's selection of men of genuine faith and integrity and by the revelation of truth to them through angelic ministrations; second, by the establishment of a

---
[1]Moroni 7:31-32.

The Prophet Joseph Smith painted by a W. Majors during the Prophet's lifetime. Owned by the Reorganized Church, the painting hangs in Independence, Missouri.

testimony of divine truth witnessed to and testified of by those ministered unto; third, by the proclamation of that testimony and truth, accompanied by the powers of the Holy Spirit, as a foundation upon which others may build true faith; and fourth, by the bestowal of the Holy Ghost upon all who act in faith and in righteousness upon the testimony they receive, by which they may know for themselves concerning the truth of God and the divinity of his work in their day. In this way, the formula of true spiritual growth is preserved and the gifts and graces of God, as given to man, are granted largely as a result of man's righteous desires and free initiative.

This formula was strictly adhered to in the establishment of the latter-day dispensation. Witnesses were raised up in the persons of Joseph Smith and others; divine truths and evidences were given; and a promise made that the Holy Ghost would bear witness of the truth to all men who would apply faith and act in righteousness upon the testimony that was given. An early revelation to Joseph Smith declares:

> And the testimony of three witnesses will I send forth of my word. And behold, whosoever believeth on my words, them will I visit with the manifestation of my Spirit; and they shall be born of me, even of water and of the Spirit.[2]

The Book of Mormon, as God's latter-day witness of divine truth, is filled with accounts of the ministry of angels. By this means a prophetic vision was revealed to Nephi;[3] and his brother, Jacob, was informed that Jerusalem had been destroyed and the Jews taken into captivity.[4] From an angel Jacob also learned that the Redeemer's name would

---

[2]Doctrine and Covenants 5:15-16. See also Alma 12:28-30; 13:22-26.
[3]1 Nephi 11:11-14.
[4]2 Nephi 6:8-9. See also 1 Nephi 7:13-14.

be Christ.⁵   An angel gave the text of a great gospel discourse to King Benjamin.⁶   Alma, having been converted
and raised up as a witness of God's mercy by an angel, was
later ministered unto by the same personage.⁷   From this
source Alma also received an explanation of certain gospel
truths.⁸   Amulek was prepared by an angel to assist Alma
in preaching the gospel;⁹ and because of the ministry of
angels large numbers of the Lamanites were converted at a
later date, by the preaching of Nephi and Lehi.¹⁰   Samuel
the Lamanite was commissioned by an angel to preach repentance to the Nephites, to warn them of coming judgments, and to foretell the birth of Christ.¹¹   As Christ's
birth drew near, angels appeared and declared the glad
tidings unto men.¹²   And when the Nephites turned again
to wickedness, after the signs of his birth had been manifested, Nephi was visited daily by heavenly messengers,
as he preached repentance and sought to prepare the people for the Lord's appearance upon the Western Hemis-
phere.¹³   That glorious appearance among the Nephites
was accompanied by the ministry of angels.¹⁴

As with many other gospel truths, men have mysti-
fied, falsely spiritualized, and then rejected the reality of
angelic ministrations.   But in the restoration of all things,
the ministry of angels was again enjoyed by those with
living faith.   Particularly was this true of Joseph Smith.
"He was visited constantly by angels," said George Q.
Cannon.¹⁵   Not only did Moroni appear unto the Prophet

⁵2 Nephi 10:3.
⁶Mosiah 3.
⁷Mosiah 27; Alma 8:14, 36.
⁸Alma 40:11-24.
⁹Alma 8:20; 10:7-9; 11:31.
¹⁰Helaman 5.
¹¹*Ibid.*, 14:9, 26, 28.
¹²*Ibid.*, 16:14.
¹³3 Nephi 7:15-18.
¹⁴*Ibid.*, 17:24; 19:14.
¹⁵*J. D.*, XXIII, p. 362.

from time to time, but other heavenly beings visited him
before he was privileged to obtain the plates. Joseph made
this fact clear when he wrote in his letter to John Wentworth: "After having received many visits *from the angels
of God* unfolding the majesty and glory of the events that
should transpire in the last days, on the morning of the 22nd
of September, A. D. 1827, the angel of the Lord delivered
the records into my hands."[16]   The Prophet's associates
also made reference to these other early visits.   John Taylor
stated that "when Joseph Smith was raised up as a Prophet
of God, Mormon, Moroni, Nephi, and others of the ancient
Prophets who formerly lived on this Continent . . . came to
him and communicated to him certain principles pertaining
to the Gospel."[17]   Again, after stating that he was merely
repeating what the Prophet had told him, John Taylor said
that after the appearance of Moroni, "then came Nephi."[18]
Orson Pratt also reported that "during those four years
[1823-1827] he [Joseph Smith] was often ministered to by
the *angels* of God, and received instructions concerning the
work that was to be performed in the latter days."[19]   George
Q. Cannon has stated:

> If you read the history of the Church from the
> beginning, you will find that Joseph was visited by
> various angelic beings, but not one of them pro-
> fessed to give him the keys until John the Baptist
> came to him.   Moroni, who held the keys of the
> record of the stick of Ephraim, visited Joseph; he
> had doubtless, also, visits from Nephi and it may
> be from Alma and others, but though they came
> and had authority, holding the authority of the
> Priesthood, we have no account of their ordaining
> him.[20]

[16]*History of the Church,* IV, p. 537. (Italics by the writer.)
[17]*J. D.,* XVII, p. 374.
[18]*Ibid.,* XXI, p. 161.
[19]*Ibid.,* XV, p. 185. (Italics by the writer.) See also XIII, p. 66.
[20]*Ibid.,* XIII, p. 47.

During the period Joseph Smith possessed the plates, he received many visitations from Moroni. John the Baptist also appeared and conferred the Aaronic Priesthood upon him and Oliver Cowdery. Later, Peter, James, and John restored the holy apostleship to the earth.[21]

The appearance of John the Baptist occurred after Joseph Smith and Oliver Cowdery had gone "into the woods to pray and inquire of the Lord respecting baptism for the remission of sins," as they found it mentioned in the Nephite record.[22] Oliver Cowdery explained that they had by then translated the account of Christ's appearance among the Nephites and the instructions he then gave on baptism. While they were inquiring concerning baptism, the Prophet's companion later wrote,

On a sudden, as from the midst of eternity, the voice of the Redeemer spoke peace to us. While the veil was parted and the angel of God came down clothed with glory, and delivered the anxiously looked for message, and the keys of the Gospel of repentance. What joy! what wonder! what amazement! While the world was racked and distracted—while millions were groping as the blind for the wall, and while all men were resting upon uncertainty, as a general mass, our eyes beheld, our ears heard, as in the "blaze of day"; yes, more—above the glitter of the May sunbeam, which then shed its brilliancy over the face of nature! Then his voice, though mild, pierced to the center, and his words, "I am thy fellow-servant," dispelled every fear. We listened, we gazed, we admired! 'Twas the voice of an angel, from glory, 'twas a message from the Most High! And as we heard we rejoiced, while His love enkindled upon our souls, and we were wrapped in the vision of the Almighty! Where

---

[21]To Joseph Smith and Oliver Cowdery.
[22]*History of the Church*, I, pp. 39-41.

was room for doubt?   Nowhere; uncertainty had
fled, doubt had sunk no more to rise, while fiction
and deception had fled forever. . . .

I shall not attempt to paint to you the feelings
of this heart, nor the majestic beauty and glory
which surrounded us on this occasion; but you will
believe me when I say, that earth, nor men, with
the eloquence of time, cannot begin to clothe language in as interesting and sublime a manner as
this holy personage.   No; nor has this earth power
to give the joy, to bestow the peace, or comprehend the wisdom which was contained in each
sentence as they were delivered by the power of
the Holy Spirit!   Man may deceive his fellow men,
deception may follow deception, and the children
of the wicked may have power to seduce the foolish and untaught, till naught but fiction feeds the
many, and the fruit of falsehood carries in its cur-
rent the giddy to the grave; but one touch with
the finger of His love, yes, one ray of glory from
the upper world, or one word from the mouth of
the Savior, from the bosom of eternity, strikes it all
into insignificance, and blots it forever from the
mind.   The assurance that we were in the presence
of an angel, the certainty that we heard the voice
of Jesus, and the truth unsullied as it flowed from a
pure personage, dictated by the will of God, is to
me past description, and I shall ever look upon
this expression of the Savior's goodness with wonder and thanksgiving while I am permitted to
tarry; and in those mansions where perfection
dwells and sin never comes, I hope to adore in that
day which shall never cease.[23]

John the Baptist explained "that he acted under the
direction of Peter, James and John who held the keys of
the Priesthood of Melchizedek," and promised that they
would in due time receive that priesthood.[24]   According to

---

[23]*Times and Seasons*, II, p. 201.
[24]*History of the Church*, I, pp. 39-41.

existing evidence the promised ordination occurred shortly thereafter. In April, 1830, a revelation stated that Joseph Smith had been called of God and "ordained an apostle of Jesus Christ," and that Oliver Cowdery was also "called of God an apostle of Jesus Christ."[25] Another revelation spoke of "Peter, and James, and John, whom I have sent unto you, by whom I have ordained you and confirmed you to be apostles."[26] Though the exact date of this ordination is not known, it probably came before July, 1829, for a revelation in June referred to Oliver Cowdery and David Whitmer as being called with the same calling as the Apostle Paul.[27] The ordination to the Melchizedek Priesthood occurred "in the wilderness between Harmony, Susquehanna County, and Colesville, Broome County, [Pennsylvania], on the Susquehanna river."[28]

Oliver Cowdery gave several testimonies of the above visitations by John the Baptist and by Peter, James, and John. In an address at Council Bluffs, Iowa, October 29, 1848, he testified that he "was present with Joseph Smith when an holy angel from God came down from heaven and conferred on us, or restored, the lesser or Aaronic Priesthood." He also declared that he was "present with Joseph Smith when the higher or Melchizedek Priesthood was conferred."[29] Over two years earlier he wrote in a personal letter:

---

[25]Doctrine and Covenants 20:2-3.
[26]*Ibid.*, 27:12-13. See also 5:6; 21:10-11; 43:7; 113:5-6; 124:57-58.
[27]*Ibid.*, 18:9. Brigham Young referred to Oliver Cowdery and David Whitmer as being apostles. See *J. D.*, VI, p. 320.
[28]Doctrine and Covenants 128:20.
[29]Published in *Deseret News*, April 13, 1859. In a letter written from Cambridge Port, U.S.A., December 26, 1848, to Orson Pratt in England, Wilford Woodruff reported that Orson Hyde was present when Cowdery made this address and that Hyde had subsequently written to him [Woodruff] concerning it. Pratt published Woodruff's letter in the *Millennial Star*, XI (February 1, 1849), p. 43. George A. Smith who was also present at Council Bluffs wrote to Orson Pratt, October 31, 1848, stating: "He [Cowdery] bore testimony in the most positive terms of the truth of the Book of Mormon—the restoration of the Priesthood to the earth, and the mission of Joseph Smith as the Prophet of the last days." This letter was also published in the *Millennial Star*, XI (January 1, 1849), p. 14.

I have cherished a hope, and that one of my fondest, that I might leave such a character, as those who might believe in my testimony, after I should be called hence, might do so, not only for the sake of truth, but might not *blush* for the private character of the man who bore that testimony. I have been sensitive on this subject, I admit, but I ought to be so—you would be, under the circumstances, had you stood in the presence of *John,* with your departed brother Joseph, to receive the lesser Priesthood—and in the presence of Peter to receive the greater, and looked down through time, and witnessed the effects these two must produce, you would feel what you have never felt.[30]

Evidence supports the conclusion that Joseph Smith and Oliver Cowdery told others of these ordinations at an early date. Pomeroy Tucker, an early resident of Palmyra, expressed his antagonism to their claims when he wrote:

He [Joseph Smith] now arrogated to himself, by authority of "the spirit of revelation," and in accordance with the previous "promises" made to him [by John the Baptist ?], a far higher sphere in the scale of human existence, assuming to possess the gift and power of "prophet, seer, and revelator [the presiding office in the Melchizedek Priesthood]." . . . This was substantially, if not literally, the pretension of Smith, as related by himself, and repeatedly quoted by his credulous friends at the time.[31]

In November, 1830, the *Painesville Telegraph*, Painesville, Ohio, reported the arrival in that area of Oliver

---

[30]Letter written by Oliver Cowdery, March 23, 1846, Tiffin, Seneca County, Ohio, to Phineas Young. Original in Church Historian's Office, Salt Lake City, Utah.

[31]Pomeroy Tucker, *Origin, Rise and Progress of Mormonism* (New York, 1867), p. 29.

Cowdery and others, as missionaries of the restored gospel. In its report the *Telegraph* commented that one of the missionaries "pretends to have seen angels." The use of the plural term indicates that Cowdery claimed ministrations from other angels than Moroni—presumably John the Baptist, Peter, James, and John. Continued the *Telegraph*: "The name of the person here, who pretends to have a divine mission and to have seen and conversed with angels is Cowdery."[32] A few months later the *Palmyra Reflector*, Palmyra, New York, carried an article on Mormonism, in which it gave a report from its Painesville, Ohio, correspondent of Mormon activities in that area. Said the *Reflector*, "Cowdery and his friends had frequent interviews with angels."[33]

The appearance of Peter, James, and John to restore the Melchizedek Priesthood and the key of the apostleship was not the only time that members of that ancient Presidency made their appearance among men in these last days. On more than one occasion, Heber C. Kimball declared that when the Twelve were anointed in the Kirtland Temple "John stood in their midst," while Peter was "in the stand." Kimball later declared that he could "bring twenty witnesses" who beheld the ancient personages.[34] Later, when the Prophet was in Missouri, he reportedly stated that he had "a conversation a few days ago" with the Apostle Peter.[35]

---

[32]*Painesville Telegraph*, November 16, 1830.
[33]*Palmyra Reflector*, February 14, 1831.
[34]Minutes of the School of the Prophets, held at Provo, Utah, May 18, 1868. Brigham Young University Library; *J. D.*, IX, p. 376; Whitney, *op. cit.*, IX, p. 130. During a conference held June 3, 1831, Joseph Smith declared "that John the Revelator was then among the ten tribes of Israel who had been led away by Shalmaneser, king of Assyria, to prepare them for their return from that long dispersion."—Joseph Fielding Smith, *Essentials in Church History*, (Salt Lake City, 1947), p. 126.
[35]"The Reed Peck Manuscript," handwritten account of incidents during the Missouri era of Mormon history, dated September 18, 1839. Taken from a photostat of the original, Brigham Young University Library, pp. 25-26, 54-55.

The temple at Kirtland, Ohio, was built primarily that important keys pertaining to the priesthood might be restored to earth through angelic ministrations and that the Saints might receive a pentacostal endowment like that which the New Testament Saints received. The promised endowment was to be an important landmark in developing the spiritual foundations of this dispensation. Before the Prophet moved Church headquarters from New York to Ohio, a revelation, dated January 2, 1831, promised that in their new location they were to "be endowed with power from on high."[36] Three days later another revelation promised that if the Church would assemble in Ohio, the members would receive "a blessing such as is not known among men, and it shall be poured forth upon their heads."[37] In February, 1831, after the Prophet had arrived in Ohio, a revelation promised, "And ye are to be taught from on high. Sanctify yourselves and ye shall be endowed with power."[38]

In June, 1833, a revelation designated the temple as the place where the anticipated Pentecost would occur, declaring: "Yea, verily I say unto you, I give unto you a commandment that you should build a house, in the which house I design to endow those whom I have chosen with power from on high; for this is the promise of the Father unto you; therefore I command you to tarry, even as mine apostles at Jerusalem."[39] When the Twelve Apostles were called and ordained, in the early months of 1835, they were told that they must cross "the mighty deep" and preach the gospel to other nations. But, said Oliver Cowdery in the apostolic charge, "You are not to go to other nations till you receive your endowments. . . . You need a fountain

---

[36]Doctrine and Covenants 38:32.
[37]Ibid., 39:15.
[38]Ibid., 43:16.
[39]Ibid., 95:8-9.

of wisdom, knowledge and intelligence such as you never had."[40]

From that time forward the Prophet worked industriously to prepare the Saints for the endowment. In March, 1835, the school in Kirtland closed, "to give the Elders an opportunity to go forth and proclaim the Gospel, preparatory to the endowment."[41] Labor in the ministry would assist them to develop the needed humility for that blessing. Heretofore the Prophet had been able to bring but one or two, or at the most but few, to the point of faith and humility necessary to behold with him the visions and powers of God. Now the Church was to be offered this blessing; but it would take preparation. In October, 1835, he admonished the Twelve "to prepare their hearts in all humility for an endowment with power from on high."[42] The following month a revelation reproved that quorum for their weaknesses and declared, "Verily I say unto you, they must all humble themselves before me, before they will be accounted worthy to receive an endowment."[43]

In a letter to his wife, December 18, 1835, William W. Phelps expressed the desires of the Saints at the time when he wrote, "Keep up your faith and pray for the endowment."[44] The following month he again wrote to her telling of a meeting held January 17th:

> At an early hour, all authorities of the Church regularly organized, met in the school room under our printing office, and the presidents commenced the meeting by confessing their sins and forgiving their brethren and the world. . . . The Lord poured out His Spirit in such a manner

---

[40]*History of the Church*, II, p. 197.
[41]*Ibid.*, p. 218.
[42]*Ibid.*, p. 287.
[43]*Ibid.*, p. 300.
[44]*Journal History*, December 18, 1835.

as you never witnessed. When I was speaking, which was but few words, the Spirit of the Lord came upon me so that I could not speak, and I cried as little children cry in earnest, and the tears from my eyes ran in streams; the audience, which was the largest ever convened in the said room, sobbed and wept aloud. The Presidency and the "Twelve" occupied the forenoon. There was speaking and singing in tongues and prophesying as on the day of Pentecost.[45]

During the following week certain of the brethren received the initial ordinances of the endowment, during which the Prophet reported:

The heavens were opened upon us, and I beheld the celestial kingdom of God, and the glory thereof, whether in the body or out I cannot tell. I saw the transcendent beauty of the gate through which the heirs of that kingdom will enter, which was like unto circling flames of fire; also the blazing throne of God, whereon was seated the Father and the Son. I saw the beautiful streets of that kingdom, which had the appearance of being paved with gold. I saw Father Adam and Abraham, and my father and mother, my brother, Alvin, that has long since slept. . . .[46]

After relating several other things that he then saw in vision, the Prophet said:

Many of my brethren . . . saw glorious visions also. Angels ministered unto them as well as to myself, and the power of the Highest rested upon us, the house was filled with the glory of God, and we shouted Hosanna to God and the Lamb. My scribe also received his anointing with us, and saw, in a vision, the armies of heaven protecting the

---

[45]*Ibid.,* January 17, 1836.
[46]*History of the Church,* II, p. 380.

Saints in their return to Zion, and many things which I saw.[47]

These were but preliminary developments leading up to the endowment that came in March and April of that year. Preparations for the greater event still continued. During the evening of January 24th, "the Prophet met the Presidency in the chamber over the printing room and counseled on the subject of [the] endowment and the preparation for the solemn assembly, which was to be called when the house of the Lord was finished."[48] Later, as Joseph wrote the prayer that was to be offered at the dedication, he included the following supplication:

> Let the anointing of thy ministers be sealed upon them with power from on high. Let it be fulfilled upon them, as upon those on the day of Pentecost; let the gift of tongues be poured out upon thy people, even cloven tongues as of fire, and the interpretation thereof. And let thy house be filled, as with a rushing mighty wind, with thy glory.[49]

When the Kirtland Temple was dedicated, on March 27, 1836, the Saints began to realize in abundance the blessings of the long-anticipated endowment. During the day Frederick G. Williams and David Whitmer testified to the appearance of heavenly messengers.[50] That evening, as George A. Smith arose to speak, the Prophet reported that

> A noise was heard like the sound of a rushing mighty wind, which filled the Temple, and all the congregation simultaneously arose, being

[47]*Ibid.*, p. 381.
[48]*Journal History*, January 24, 1836.
[49]Doctrine and Covenants 109:35-37.
[50]*History of the Church*, II, p. 427; Whitney, *op. cit.*, IX, p. 130.

moved upon by an invisible power; many began to speak in tongues and prophesy; others saw glorious visions; and I beheld the Temple was filled with angels, which fact I declared to the congregation. The people of the neighborhood came running together (hearing an unusual sound within, and seeing a bright light like a pillar of fire resting upon the Temple), and were astonished at what was taking place. This continued until the meeting closed at eleven p.m.[51]

Other meetings, with similar manifestations, followed. On April 3, 1836, Christ appeared in glory in open vision to Joseph Smith and Oliver Cowdery, followed by Moses, Elias, and Elijah, who bestowed the keys of their priesthood upon the Prophet and his associate. Of these divine commissions, Joseph wrote:

> . . . the heavens were again opened unto us; and Moses appeared before us, and committed unto us the keys of the gathering of Israel from the four parts of the earth, and the leading of the ten tribes from the land of the north. After this, Elias appeared, and committed the dispensation of the gospel of Abraham, saying that in us and our seed all generations after us should be blessed.

[51]*History of the Church,* II, p. 428. Accounts by others present agree with the above. Heber C. Kimball wrote: "March 27, 1836. . . . . I received many manifestations of the power of God, and participated in all the blessings and ordinances of endowment, which were then administered."—*Journal History,* under date. George A. Smith declared that "hundreds of brethren" had participated in "a greater manifestation of the power of God than that described by Luke on the day of Pentecost."—*J. D.,* II, p. 215. On another occasion he described the event, stating that "there came a shock on the house like a sound of a mighty rushing wind."—*J. D.,* II, p. 10. John Tanner wrote that he was present and "took part in the 'solemn assembly' and the glorious gifts and manifestations of that memorial occasion."—*Scraps of Biography:Tenth Book,* ed. A. H. Cannon (Salt Lake City, 1883), p. 14. Jedediah M. Grant "participated . . . in the great manifestations of the power and glory of God, which characterized" these events. —*The Contributor,* IV, p. 242. And Milo Andrus wrote: "I was in Kirtland at the dedication of the Temple and the endowment of the Elders. . . . I saw fire descend and rest on the heads of the Elders, and they spoke with tongues, and prophesied."—"Autobiographical Sketch," published by the Andrus family under title of *Milo Andrus Genealogy,* p. 4.

After this vision had closed, another great
and glorious vision burst upon us; for Elijah the
prophet, who was taken to heaven without tasting
death, stood before us, and said: Behold, the time
has fully come, which was spoken of by the mouth
of Malachi, testifying that he [Elijah] should be
sent, before the great and dreadful day of the Lord
come—to turn the hearts of the fathers to the
children, and the children to the fathers, lest the
whole earth be smitten with a curse. Therefore,
the keys of this dispensation are committed into
your hands; and by this ye may know that the
great and dreadful day of the Lord is near, even
at the doors.[52]

Joseph Smith received visitations from several ancient
prophets, including Adam, the patriarch of the human
family. Said John Taylor, "If you were to ask Joseph what
sort of a looking man Adam was, he would tell you at once;
he would tell you his size and appearance and all about
him."[53] The Prophet compared his oldest brother, Alvin,
with Adam and Seth, saying that Alvin "was a very handsome man, surpassed by none other but Adam and Seth,
and of great strength."[54] Again, Joseph spoke of Adam as
"such a perfect man, great and stout, that he never stumbled
or fell a joint [sic] to the ground."[55]

Zebedee Coltrin reported having been with the Prophet and Oliver Cowdery when they "saw the heaven open
and in it a great golden throne and on it a man and woman
with hair as white as snow." They were told by Joseph
that "the man and woman was Father Adam and [Mother]
Eve."[56] On another occasion Joseph Smith expressed his

---

[52]Doctrine and Covenants 110:11-16.
[53]J. D., XVIII, p. 326.
[54]History of the Church, V, p. 347.
[55]Statement made in presence of Dimick Huntington, "Diary of Oliver B.
Huntington, 1847-1900," Part II, p. 207. Brigham Young University Library.
[56]As related by Coltrin to Huntington, ibid., p. 244.

familiarity with the Ancient of Days. At the time he was going on a mission to Upper Canada and had stopped in Pennsylvania at the home of a member of the Church. This brother's wife had been given a remarkable spiritual manifestation, in which she saw a glorious personage. As she described the personage to the Prophet, she asked him to confirm whether the vision came from God or from some other source. Joseph declared that it came from God and that the personage she saw was undoubtedly Michael the Archangel, or Adam, adding that he had seen him "several times."[57]

The Prophet had considerable to say about Adam's priesthood authority. Said he, "Adam holds the keys of the dispensation of the fullness of times; i. e., the dispensation of all the times have been and will be revealed through him from the beginning to Christ, and from Christ to the end of the dispensations that are to be revealed." Whenever the priesthood is restored, it is by the authority of Adam, who in turn acts under the direction of Jesus Christ.[58] While exercising that authority, the Ancient of Days blessed his posterity and set the mold for prophetic events from the dawn of history to the end of time. This Joseph Smith was shown in vision, and he reported:

> I saw Adam in the valley of Adam-ondi-Ahman. He called together his children and blessed them with a patriarchal blessing. The Lord appeared in their midst, and he (Adam) blessed them all, and foretold what should befall them to the lastest generation.[59]

---

[57]Related by Daniel Tyler, *Juvenile Instructor*, XXVII, p. 93. Tyler's mother was the woman who received the manifestation.
[58]See *History of the Church*, IV, pp. 207-212, 383-392.
[59]Doctrine and Covenants 107:53-57; *History of the Church*, III, p. 388. The Prophet probably received this vision December 18, 1833 when he, as the first patriarch in this dispensation, bestowed a blessing upon the head of his father, "while the visions of the Almighty were open to his view."—See Joseph Fielding Smith, *Church History and Modern Revelation* (Salt Lake City, 1953), I, pp. 473-474.

Adam played an important role in the latter-day restoration of the gospel. Aside from the above-mentioned communications, "the voice of Michael" was heard by the Prophet "on the banks of the Susquehanna, detecting the devil when he appeared as an angel of light." From him the latter-day seer also received certain keys of the priesthood pertaining to the first dispensation of the gospel over which Adam presided.[60] In the future, before the appearance of Christ in glory, the Ancient of Days will sit in the valley of Adam-ondi-Ahman, as foreseen by Daniel the prophet.[61] Of that event Joseph Smith said:

Daniel in his seventh chapter speaks of the Ancient of Days; he means the oldest man, our Father Adam, Michael, he will call his children together and hold a council with them to prepare them for the coming of the Son of Man. He (Adam) is the father of the human family, and presides over the spirits of all men, and all that have had the keys must stand before him in this grand council. . . . The Son of Man stands before him, and there is given him glory and dominion. Adam delivers up his stewardship to Christ, that which was delivered to him as holding the keys of the universe, but retains his standing as head of the human family.[62]

In vision the Prophet saw Adam admitting the faithful into the celestial kingdom, as he exercised the keys of his eternal priesthood.[63] After beholding the Twelve Apostles of this dispensation rise by their faithfulness to the celestial kingdom and to their reward therein, the Prophet beheld that

---

[60]Doctrine and Covenants 128:20-21.
[61]See ibid., 116.
[62]History of the Church, III, pp. 386-387.
[63]J. D., IX, p. 41.

. . . there Father Adam stood and opened the gate to them, and as they entered, he embraced them one by one and kissed them. He then led them to the throne of God, and then the Savior embraced each one of them and kissed them, and crowned each one of them in the presence of God. . . . The impression this vision left on Brother Joseph's mind was of so acute a nature, that he never could refrain from weeping while rehearsing it.[64]

Others who ministered to Joseph Smith were the three Nephites. Heber C. Kimball reported the appearance of one of them to the Prophet in the early days of the Church, near the Hill Cumorah.[65] Later, Kimball's wife, Vilate, wrote informing her husband that Joseph had received "a visit from one of the Nephites" and had been informed of things that would shortly transpire in America and in the British Isles.[66] The Prophet is also reported to have seen the three Nephites when the Saints were making a defense of Far West.[67]

In an epistle to the Saints, Joseph Smith declared that all the ancient prophets who held specific keys and powers in the priesthood had restored their respective rights and authority in this dispensation. In referring to this fact he wrote: "And again, what do we hear? . . . the voice of Michael, the archangel; the voice of Gabriel, and of Raphael, *and of divers angels, from Michael or Adam to the present time,* all declaring their dispensaton, their rights, their keys, their honors, their majesty and glory, and the power of their priesthood; giving line upon line, precept upon precept; here a little and there a little; giving us con-

---

[64]As reported by Heber C. Kimball. Whitney, *op. cit.,* IX, p. 130. See also *History of the Church,* II, p. 381.
[65]Minutes of the School of the Prophets, held at Provo, Utah, May 18, 1868.
[66]Whitney, *op. cit.,* X, p. 138.
[67]"Diary of Oliver B. Huntington," *op. cit.,* p. 162.

solation by holding forth that which is to come, confirming our hope!"[68] While discussing the subject of the restoration of the gospel in this dispensation, John Taylor later spoke on the same theme and said:

> I know of what I speak for I was very well acquainted with him [Joseph] and was with him a great deal during his life, and was with him when he died. The principles which he had, placed him in communication with the Lord, and not only with the Lord, but with the ancient apostles and prophets; such men, for instance, as Abraham, Isaac, Jacob, Noah, Adam, Seth, Enoch, and Jesus and the Father, and the apostles that lived on this continent as well as those who lived on the Asiatic continent.[69]

"He seemed to be as familiar with these people as we are with one another," President Taylor continued, as he pointed to the fact that all these manifestations were necessary that the Dispensation of the Fulness of Times might be ushered in—"a dispensation in which all other dispensations are merged or concentrated."[70] William Taylor, after spending considerable time with Joseph Smith, corroborated his brother's testimony when he said of the Prophet, "He seemed to be just as familiar with the Spirit World, and as well acquainted with the other side, as he was here."[71] Said John Taylor on another occasion:

> Although the Church was so few in number the principles and purposes of God were developed fully to the vision of his [Joseph's] mind, and he gazed upon the things that are to trans-

---

[68]Doctrine and Covenants 128:21. (Italics by the writer.) Gabriel is Noah. See *History of the Church,* III, p. 386. The identity of Raphael is not known.
[69]J. D., XXI, p. 94. See *ibid.,* p. 65, where he makes specific reference to the appearance of Enoch.
[70]*Idem.*
[71]*Young Woman's Journal,* XVII, p. 548.

pire in the latter-days associated with the dispensation that he was called upon by the Almighty to introduce. He learned by communication from the heavens, from time to time, of the great events that should transpire in the latter days. He understood things that were past, and comprehended the various dispensations and the designs of those dispensations. He not only had the principles developed, but he was conversant with the parties who officiated as the leading men of those dispensations, and from a number of them he received authority and keys and priesthood and power for the carrying out of the great purposes of the Lord in the last days, who were sent and commissioned specially by the Almighty to confer upon him those keys and this authority, and hence he introduced what was spoken of by all the prophets since the world was; the dispensation in which we live which differs from all other dispensations in that it is the dispensation of the fulness of times, embracing all other dispensations, all other powers, all other keys and all other privileges and immunities that ever existed upon the face of the earth.[72]

The Prophet said much about angels and other ministering personages. He made it clear that angels of God never have wings.[73] They are not a special creation—an order of beings distinct from men. They are commissioned personages who either have come to this earth or will one day come and receive physical tabernacles. In either event, Joseph explained, "There are no angels who minister to this earth but those who do belong or have belonged to it."[74] The Prophet referred to Moroni, for example, as one who, "being dead and raised again therefrom, appeared

[72]J. D., XX, pp. 174-175.
[73]History of the Church, III, p. 392.
[74]Doctrine and Covenants 130:5.

unto me."⁷⁵   Again, he explained, "The angel that appeared to John on the Isle of Patmos was a translated or
resurrected body [i.e., personage]."⁷⁶   That being express-
ly declared to John that he was one of "the prophets."⁷⁷

Though the term *angel* is used to designate various
kinds of heavenly beings, there is a "difference between an
angel and a ministering spirit." The Prophet taught that
the first is "a resurrected or translated body, with its spirit
ministering to embodied spirits—the other a disembodied
spirit, visiting and minstering to disembodied spirits."
Jesus became a ministering spirit to the spirits in prison,
while his body was in the grave, and thus he fulfilled an
important part of his mission. After his resurrection he
went "to minister to resurrected bodies." While spirits
generally minister to other spirits, they may at times appear
unto men in mortality. But on such occasions they "can
only be revealed in flaming fire and glory," as they have
no tabernacle to hide the light. Said the Prophet, "The
spirits of just men are made ministering servants to those
who are sealed unto life eternal, and it is through them that
the sealing power comes down."⁷⁸

Heavenly messengers participate in many other functions. They engage in the latter-day gathering of the elect,
work to bring about the destruction of the wicked, preside
over the final overthrow of wickedness, minister to planets
of terrestrial glory, and in other ways carry out the mandates
of the Almighty. Joseph Smith seemed perfectly familiar
with these things, even to such matters of detail as contained in the following incident which he reported:

A man came to me in Kirtland, and told me
he had seen an angel, and described his dress. I

---

⁷⁵*History of the Church*, III, p. 28.
⁷⁶*Ibid.*, IV, p. 425.
⁷⁷Revelation 19:10; 22:9.
⁷⁸*History of the Church*, III, p. 392; IV, p. 425; VI, pp. 50-52.

told him he had seen no angel, and that there was no such dress in heaven. He grew mad, and went into the street, and commanded fire to come down out of heaven to consume me. I laughed at him, and said, "You are one of Baal's prophets; your God does not hear you; jump up and cut yourself"; and he commanded fire from heaven to consume my house.[79]

The Prophet felt that unbelieving men should accept intelligently the reality of organized life beyond the mortal sphere; and he gave three grand keys by which good or bad angels or spirits may be distinguished.[80] Such beings, he asserted, had played an active role in the restoration of the gospel and should continually minister in the proper channels unto righteous men that the divine purposes of God might be carried out in the earth.

[79]*The Historical Record, op. cit.*, p. 508; *History of the Church*, V, pp. 267-268. See also *ibid.*, II, pp. 260, 270-271; IV, pp. 207-212; J. D., IX, p. 91; XVII, p. 148; Doctrine and Covenants 76:87-88; 77:8-9; 86.

[80]See Doctrine and Covenants 129.

V.

Joseph Smith the Seer

Joseph Smith had a keen sense of discernment. By nature he possessed great powers of penetration and analysis. "I felt when in his presence that he could read me through and through," said Jesse M. Smith.[1] Bathsheba W. Smith reported a case in point:

> I used to go very often to Brother Joseph's house, though not much before I was married. Once at dinner, I knew he was looking at me, but I did not feel afraid because I knew I had always been good and obedient, and had all the faith possible in him and Mormonism, so I just let him look at me. Pretty soon he said to my sister-in-law, "George hit the right stick when he got her." And I have proved it, for my husband and I have lived happily together—like lovers.[2]

But the Prophet was more than a man of keen insight. It was foretold that he would be a "choice seer," blessed with the gift and power of seership to a remarkable degree.[3] A seer is one who *sees*, as the faculty of sight is quickened and spiritualized by the Holy Spirit. Reference has been made in a previous chapter to the fact that the gift of seership was utilized by Moroni in his instructions to the Prophet. By this gift Joseph Smith translated the Book of Mormon, through the medium of the Urim and Thummim. Through that medium he was given *"sight* and power to translate."[4]

---

[1]*Juvenile Instructor*, XXVII, pp. 23-24.
[2]*Ibid.*, p. 549.
[3]2 Nephi 3:7.
[4]Doctrine and Covenants 3:12. (Italics by the writer.)

—*Courtesy of BYU Library, owner of the original*

Pen sketch of the Prophet Joseph Smith, signed Por. S. Maudsley, Nauvoo, 1844.

The Urim and Thummim was a specially prepared instrument into which one could "*look* and translate all records that are of ancient date," wrote a Book of Mormon figure, adding, "Whosoever is commanded *to look* in them, the same is called seer."[5] The record of Abraham is also significant in establishing the fact that through the Urim and Thummim the seer could see the things revealed unto him. Said the father of the faithful: "I, Abraham, had the Urim and Thummim, which the Lord my God had given unto me, in Ur of the Chaldees; *and I saw the stars,* that they were very great, and that one of them was nearest unto the throne of God."[6]

Just how the Prophet translated is not known. It is certain, however, that it required great mental as well as spiritual powers.[7] It was not merely a matter of looking into the Urim and Thummim. On the other hand, the process was not purely mental. The gift of seership and the power of God were necessary factors in the process. Accounts by those present when the Prophet was translating support this conclusion. The *Rochester Gem,* of Rochester, New York, quoted Martin Harris as explaining that by placing the Urim and Thummim in "a hat and looking into it, Smith interprets the characters into the English language."[8] Again, Martin Harris explained that

---

[5]Mosiah 8:13. (Italics by the writer.) Compare the words of Alma: "I will prepare my servant Gazelem, a stone, which shall shine forth in darkness unto light, that I may discover unto them the works of their brethren."—Alma 37:23.

[6]Abraham 3:1-2. (Italics by the writer.) A Urim and Thummim is material endowed by and organized in union with celestial powers of truth and light. "The place where God resides is a great Urim and Thummim," the Prophet explained. That celestial sphere is made so by endowing the elements thereof with powers of intelligence to the extent that they, organized in union with his Spirit that emanates from his presence and pervades all things, reflect visually a picture of all that is transpiring in his vast dominion. Even a sparrow does not fall except the Father is aware of it. The Prophet taught further that "this earth, in its sanctified and immortal state, will be made like unto crystal and will be a Urim and Thummim to the inhabitants who dwell thereon, whereby all things pertaining to an inferior kingdom, or all kingdoms of a lower order, will be manifest to those who dwell on it."—Doctrine and Covenants 130:7-9.

[7]See Doctrine and Covenants 20:8-9.

[8]*Rochester Gem,* September 5, 1829. Cited in Willard Bean, *Scrapbook of Early Church History.*

"sentences would appear and were read by the Prophet and written by Martin, and when finished he would say, 'written,' and if correctly written, that sentence would disappear and another appear in its place."[9] David Whitmer gave similar explanations. Said he:

> Joseph Smith would put the seer stone into a hat, and exclude the light, and in the darkness the Spiritual light would shine. A piece of something resembling parchment would appear, and on that appeared the writing. One character at a time would appear, and under it was the interpretation in English. Brother Joseph would read off the English to Oliver Cowdery, who was his principal scribe, and when it was written down and repeated to Brother Joseph to see if it was correct, then it would disappear, and another character with the interpretation would appear.[10]

After repeating this explanation at another time, Whitmer added, "Smith, who was illiterate and but little versed in Biblical lore, was oft times compelled to spell the words out, not knowing the correct pronunciation."[11] Emma, the Prophet's wife, also admitted that he "could neither write, nor dictate a coherent and well-worded letter, let alone dictate a book like the Book Mormon," but testified, "I frequently wrote day by day, often sitting at the table close to him, he sitting with his face buried in his hat, with the stone in it, and dictating hour after hour."[12]

The Prophet used the Urim and Thummim for other

---

[9]*Deseret News*, April 13, 1859.
[10]David Whitmer, *Address to All Believers*, p. 12. See *Kansas City Journal*, June 5, 1881, for another almost identical statement by Whitmer.
[11]*Deseret News*, December 24, 1885. This may have been an accurate statement based upon the Prophet's educational status at the time, but by his efforts he later became a highly educated person.
[12]Edward W. Tullidge, *History of Joseph Smith*, pp. 794-795. See "Diary of Oliver B. Huntington," *op. cit.*, pp. 170-171, for a statement by Joseph F. Smith describing the translation of the Book of Mormon as explained by Harris, Whitmer, etc.

purposes than the translation of the Book of Mormon. Mother Smith reported that through that instrument Moroni showed Joseph "many things which he saw in vision."[13] Several revelations, now found in the Doctrine and Covenants, were given through the Urim and Thummim. It was through that instrument and by vision, independent of its agency, that most of what is termed *Mormonism* originated. The church organization Joseph Smith set up—the most perfect piece of social mechanism known to men today—was shown to him by vision. He saw the Church as it was to be organized; and as conditions permitted, he duplicated that vision on earth. Thus, he continually labored with the several quorums of the priesthood "to bring them to the order which God had shown" unto him.[14]

The organization of the Quorum of the Twelve Apostles and the First Quorum of the Seventy grew out of a vision the Prophet had received concerning the order of Church government. The minutes of the meeting at which he began the organization of the Twelve report that "President Smith then stated that the meeting had been called because God had commanded it; and *it was made known to him by vision* and by the Holy Spirit."[15] When the First Quorum of the Seventy was organized, this matter was carried out, said the Prophet, "according to the visions and revelations which I have received."[16] In a formal revelation defining the powers, responsibilities, and organizational relationships of the presiding quorums in the Church, he said of the seventy:

> . . . it is *according to the vision showing the order of the Seventy,* that they should have seven

---

[13]Lucy Mack Smith, *op. cit.,* p. 110.
[14]*History of the Church,* II, pp. 391-392.
[15]*Ibid.,* p. 181. (Italics by the writer.)
[16]*Ibid.,* pp. 201-202.

presidents to preside over them, chosen out of the number of the seventy;

And the seventh president of these presidents is to preside over the six; and these seven presidents are to choose other seventy besides the first seventy to whom they belong, and are to preside over them;

And also other seventy, until seven times seventy, if the labor in the vineyard of necessity requires it.[17]

When Joseph Smith began to set the various councils of the priesthood in order, he apparently drew from the intelligence communicated to him through vision for his understanding of how such councils should function. By vision he was shown how ancient priesthood councils were conducted, and he then set about teaching the brethren about such matters. On October 11, 1831, he instructed the brethren "in the ancient manner of conducting meetings as they were led by the Holy Ghost." Most of the elders, he commented, "were ignorant" on these matters, the obvious reason being that such information was not available except from himself, and he had not until then instructed them on these matters.[18]   Later, when he was about to organize the first high council, the Prophet again emphasized the way ancient councils functioned:

In ancient days councils were conducted with such strict propriety, that no one was allowed to whisper, be weary, leave the room, or get uneasy in the least, until the voice of the Lord, by revelation, or the voice of the council by the Spirit, was obtained, which has not been observed in this Church to the present time.   It was understood in

[17]Doctrine and Covenants 107:93-96. (Italics by the writer.)
[18]Journal History, October 11, 1831; History of the Church, I, p. 219. The Journal History indicates that this instructional meeting was to be held October 12th, while the History of the Church states it was held on the 11th.

ancient days, that if one man could stay in council,
another could; and if the president could spend his
time, the members could also; but in our councils,
generally, one will be uneasy, another asleep; one
praying, another not; one's mind on the business of
the council, and another thinking on something
else.[19]

The priesthood could not be fully organized without
a temple; and here again Joseph was largely taught by
vision. A revelation concerning the Nauvoo Temple said:
"And I will show unto my servant Joseph all things pertaining to this house, and the priesthood thereof, and the place
whereon it shall be built."[20]   Later, Joseph Smith made the
following significant entry in his *Journal*:

> In the afternoon, Elder William Weeks
> (whom I had employed as architect of the Tem-
> ple,) came in for instruction. I instructed him in
> relation to the circular windows designed to light
> the offices in the dead work of the arch between
> stories. He said that round windows in the broad
> side of a building were a violation of all the known
> rules of architecture, and contended that they
> should be semicircular—that the building was too
> low for round windows. I told him I would have
> the circles, if he had to make the Temple ten feet
> higher than it was originally calculated; that one
> light at the centre of each circular window would
> be sufficient to light the whole room; that when the
> whole building was thus illuminated, the effect
> would be remarkably grand. "I wish you to carry
> out *my designs.* I have seen in vision the splendid
> appearance of that building illuminated, and will
> have it built according to the pattern shown
> me."[21]

[19]*History of the Church,* II, pp. 25-26.
[20]Doctrine and Covenants 124:42. (Italics by writer.)
[21]*History of the Church,* VI, pp. 196-197.

Josiah Quincy reported evidence to corroborate the Prophet's statement, when he and Charles Francis Adams were shown the temple during their visit in Nauvoo. Near the entrance to the temple they passed a workman who was laboring upon a huge stone, carved to portray the face of a man.

"General Smith," said the man, looking up from his task, "is this like the face you saw in vision?"

"Very near it," answered the prophet, "except" (this was added with an air of careful connoisseurship that was quite overpowering) "except that the nose is just a thought too broad."[22]

Of the temple, Quincy said: "Being, presumably, like something Smith had seen in vision, it cannot be compared to any ecclesiastical building which may be discerned by the natural eyesight."[23] Some parts of the temple were designed according to existing architectural styles, as is apparent when one makes a study of that structure. But on the whole the design was largely original. One observer said:

> The appearance presented by this edifice in the diagram model, which was shown to me by the Prophet, is grand and imposing. The Tower, the casements, the doors, and all the prominent parts of the edifice, are to be richly ornamented, both within and without—but in a style of architecture, which no Greek, nor Goth, nor Frank, ever dreamed. I will be bound to affirm. Indeed, as I learned from the lips of the Prophet himself— the style of architecture is exclusively his own and must be known, henceforth and forever, I suppose, as the Mormon order![24]

---

[22]Quincy, op. cit., p. 389.
[23]Idem.
[24]Illinois State Register, Springfield, Illinois, IV (March 31, 1843), p. 1.

The Saints were to be organized into a society that included the plan for the ideal city. It was expected that, when Zion's organization was properly developed and regulated, there would be a bishop to each municipal organization of from fifteen to twenty thousand people; but until then, the Prophet wrote, things must be arranged "according to wisdom."[25] The more perfect plan would no doubt have to await the establishment of the full program of consecration and stewardship. Students interested in the Prophet's views on city organization have noted the uniqueness and the originality of his plan.[26] Here again he drew upon a heavenly source for that which he endeavored to develop on the earth. Several cities were to be built up according to the essential outline of the plan shown to the Prophet, including Kirtland, Ohio, and Independence, Missouri. In May, 1833, a revelation commanded the Saints to establish the "foundation of the city of the stake of Zion, here in the land of Kirtland, . . . according to the pattern which I have given unto you."[27] In reporting the proceedings of the conference held April 6, 1837, Wilford Woodruff threw further light on the origin of this plan. Said he of the Prophet's activities at that conference:

He also presented us in some degree with the plot of the city of Kirtland, which is the stronghold of the Daughter of Zion. The plan which he presented was given to him by vision, and the future will prove that the visions of Joseph concerning Jackson County, all the various stakes of Zion and of the redemption of Israel will be fulfilled in the time appointed of the Lord.[28]

---

[25]History of the Church, I, p. 368.
[26]See, for example, Lowry Nelson, The Mormon Village (Salt Lake City, 1952), p. 40.
[27]Doctrine and Covenants 94:1-2.
[28]Journal History, April 6, 1837.

During the months that preceded his martyrdom, the
Prophet felt a sense of urgency to outline in detail the plan of
the kingdom of God as it had been shown unto him, and to
confer upon the Twelve the keys and powers he had received. He said, "I know not why; but for some reason I am
constrained to hasten my preparations, and to confer upon
the Twelve all the ordinances, keys, covenants, and endowments, and sealing ordinances of the priesthood, and so set
before them a pattern in all things pertaining to the sanctu-
ary and the endowment therein." Having done so, he
rejoiced exceedingly and said, "The Lord is about to lay the
burden on your shoulders and let me rest awhile; and if
they kill me, the kingdom of God will roll on, as I have now
finished the work which was laid upon me, by committing
to you all things for the building up of the kingdom *according to the heavenly vision, and the pattern shown me
from heaven.*"[29]

The latter-day seer made repeated reference to the
visions that were continually opened to his mind. "As Paul
said, so say I," he declared; "let us come to visions and
revelations."[30]   In his *Journal* he reported, "The Spirit and
visions of God attended me through the night."[31]   He set
out to locate and to dedicate the site for the latter-day city
of Zion or New Jerusalem, in Missouri, because he had been
commanded to do so "by a heavenly vision."[32]   Shortly
thereafter he wrote to William W. Phelps, "Brother William, in the love of God, having the most implicit confidence
in you as a man of God, having obtained this confidence
by a vision of heaven, therefore I will proceed to unfold
to you some of the feelings of my heart."[33]

As Zion's Camp journeyed from Kirtland to Missouri

---

[29]*Millennial Star*, V (March, 1845), p. 151. (Italics by the writer.)
[30]*History of the Church*, II, p. 380.
[31]*Ibid.*, p. 383.
[32]*Ibid.*, p. 254.
[33]*Journal History*, November 27, 1832.

in the spring of 1834, Joseph and others visited some mounds in which the ancient inhabitants had buried their dead. In one mound they unearthed the skeleton of a large, thick-set man; and between his ribs was a stone-pointed arrow. When the brethren expressed an anxiety to know who the person was, "the Lord showed the Prophet the history of the man in a vision." His name was Zelph, a white Lamanite and a man of God. He was a warrior and chieftain under the great prophet Onandagus, who was known from the Hill Cumorah, or eastern sea, to the Rocky Mountains, and had been killed during the last great struggle of the Lamanites and Nephites.[34]

During the journey of Zion's Camp to Missouri, cholera broke out among the group and several of the brethren succumbed to the malady. The following year the Prophet related a vision to Brigham and Joseph Young, concerning the state and condition of those who died in Zion's Camp. Said he, "Brethren, I have seen those men who died of the cholera in our camp; and the Lord knows, if I get a mansion as bright as theirs, I ask no more." As he related this vision he wept "and for some time could not speak."[35]

After the Saints had been driven from Missouri and the Prophet had lain for months in prison, his gift as a seer was operative in assisting him and his brethren to make their escape. In the early part of April, 1839, he wrote, "During the night the visions of the future were opened to my understanding, when I saw the ways and means and near approach of my escape from imprisonment."[36] A few days later they realized their desires and were soon with the Saints in Illinois.

---

[34]Ibid., June 30, 1834; Times and Seasons, VI, p. 788; History of the Church, II, pp. 79-80.
[35]Joseph Young, Sr., History of the Organization of the Seventies, (Salt Lake City, 1878), pp. 1-2.
[36]Journal History, April 10, 1839.

The things the Prophet beheld in vision were many
and varied. After reading a book on the Christian martyrs,
he returned it to its owner with the comment, "I have, by
the aid of the Urim and Thummim, seen those martyrs, and
they were honest, devoted followers of Christ, according
to the light they possessed, and they will be saved."[37]   By
vision Joseph beheld that he and several of his associates
descended through related blood lines that ran back through
the aristocracy of Europe. He also beheld that they were
lawful heirs of the priesthood by birth.[38]   Furthermore, "the
women who entered into plural marriage with the Prophet
Joseph Smith were shown to him and named to him as early
as 1831." So reported Joseph F. Smith, at the time a
Counselor in the First Presidency of the Church; he added,
"And when the Lord showed those women to Joseph some
of them were not even acquainted with the Church much
less him."[39]

Many great doctrinal truths were made known to
Joseph Smith by vision. A particular case was the vision
of the three degrees of glory (which, in reality, was a series
of visions), dealing with the great plan of eternal salvation.
At the time, the Prophet and Sidney Rigdon were working
on the inspired revision of the Bible, in Hiram, Ohio, when
they came to the twenty-ninth verse of the fifth chapter of
John, concerning the resurrection of the dead. The Prophet
said, "While we meditated upon these things, the Lord
touched the eyes of our understandings and they were
opened, and the glory of the Lord shone round about."[40]
He and Sidney then beheld together the truths later recorded in that remarkable revelation.

---

[37]Stevenson, op. cit., p. 46.
[38]Reported by Heber C. Kimball, J. D., V, pp. 215-216. He stated that,
"Joseph told us these things, and I know them to be true."
[39]Journal History, February 17, 1882; Deseret News, February 17, 1882. Cited
in John A. Widtsoe, Joseph Smith, Seeker after Truth (Salt Lake City, 1951),
pp. 236-237.
[40]Doctrine and Covenants 76:15-19.

During the time this vision was revealed to Joseph and Sidney, there were other men in the room, perhaps twelve. Among these was Philo Dibble, who reported that he "saw the glory and felt the power, but did not see the vision." As he and others stood riveted to the floor, the Prophet and Sidney conversed together on the things they were beholding. Said Dibble:

> Joseph would, at intervals, say: "What do I see?" as one might say while looking out of the window and beholding what all in the room could not see. Then he would relate what he had seen or what he was looking at. Then Sidney replied, "I see the same." Presently Sidney would say, "What do I see?" and would repeat what he had seen or was seeing, and Joseph would reply, "I see the same."
>
> This manner of conversation was repeated at short intervals to the end of the vision, and during the whole time not a word was spoken by any other person. Not a sound nor motion made by anyone but Joseph and Sidney, and it seemed to me that they never moved a joint or limb during the time I was there, which I think was over an hour, and to the end of the vision.
>
> Joseph sat firmly and calmly all the time in the midst of a magnificent glory, but Sidney sat limp and pale, apparently as limber as a rag, observing which, Joseph remarked, smilingly, "Sidney is not used to it as I am."[41]

While Joseph and Sidney were still in the Spirit, they wrote a part of the great truths that had been shown to them in vision. The Prophet later stated that he "could explain a hundred fold more" than he did, were he permitted and

---

[41]*Juvenile Instructor*, XXVII, pp. 303-304. See also *Eighth Book of Faith-Promoting Series*, pp. 80-81, for another statement by Dibble.

were "the people prepared to receive them."[42] Even then some apostatized as a result of the deeper insights into man's eternal destiny, as revealed in that which was written. Said Brigham Young, "Yes, many forsook the faith when the Lord revealed the fact to Joseph Smith and Sidney Rigdon, as He did to His ancient Apostles, that all would receive a salvation except those who had sinned a sin unto death."[43] False traditions concerning but one heaven and one hell were strong. Even Brigham Young, later one of the Prophet's most stalwart supporters, confessed that he "was not prepared" at the time to say that he believed the new truths. In his mind he said, "I will wait until the Spirit of God manifests to me, for or against."[44]

From time to time thereafter Joseph Smith alluded to this vision of the glories. He said, "Paul ascended into the third heavens, and he could understand the three principal rounds of Jacob's ladder—the telestial, the terrestrial, and the celestial glories or kingdoms, where Paul saw and heard things which were not lawful for him to utter."[45] But, he explained, "Paul has seen the third heavens, and I more."[46] On another occasion he said of himself, "I know one who was caught up to the seventh heaven and saw and heard things not lawful for me to utter."[47] In a letter to James Arlington Bennett, he wrote:

> I . . . have witnessed the visions of eternity, and beheld the glorious mansions of bliss, and the regions and the misery of the damned. . . . I . . . have heard the voice of God, and communed with angels, and spake as moved by the Holy Ghost for

---

[42]*History of the Church*, V, p. 402.
[43]*J. D.*, XII, p. 105.
[44]*Ibid.*, XVIII, p. 247.
[45]*History of the Church*, V, p. 402.
[46]*The Historical Record*, op. cit., p. 514.
[47]"Journal and Memoirs of Mary Elizabeth Rollins Lightner," typewritten copy, Brigham Young University Library, p. 4.

the renewal of the Everlasting Covenant, and for
the gatherinng of Israel in the last days.[48]

On another occasion the Prophet spoke of the resurrection and said, with probable reference to the above vision:

> Would you think it strange if I relate what I
> have seen in vision in relation to this interesting
> theme? Those who have died in Jesus Christ may
> expect to enter into all that fruition of joy, when
> they come forth, which they possessed or antici-
> pated here.
>
> So plain was the vision that I actually saw
> men, before they had ascended from the tomb, as
> though they were getting up slowly. They took
> each other by the hand, and said to each other:
> "My father, my son, my mother, my daughter, my
> brother, my sister." And when the voice calls for
> the dead to arise, suppose I am laid by the side of
> my father, what would be the first joy of my heart?
> To meet my father, my mother, my brother, my
> sister; and when they are by my side, I will em-
> brace them and they me. . . .
>
> Oh! how I would delight to bring before you
> things which you never thought of! But poverty
> and the cares of the world prevent. . . . All your
> losses will be made up to you in the resurrection,
> provided you continue faithful. By the vision
> of the Almighty I have seen it.[49]

Another great vision the Prophet beheld concerned the
westward move of the Church to the Rocky Mountains.
The fact that the Saints would one day colonize the West
was known to Joseph Smith at an early date. But in August,
1842, while he and others were at Montrose, Iowa, he was

---

[48]*History of the Church*, VI, pp. 77-78.
[49]*The Historical Record*, op. cit., p. 512.

shown in vision the great exodus of the Saints. Said Anson
Call, who was present at the time:

> I had before seen him in a vision, and now saw
> while he was talking his countenance change to
> white; not the deadly white of a bloodless face, but
> a living brilliant white. He seemed absorbed in
> gazing at something at a great distance, and said:
> "I am gazing upon the valleys of those mountains."
> This was followed by a vivid description of the
> scenery of these mountains, as I have since become
> acquainted with it. Pointing to Shadrach Roundy
> and others, he said: "There are some men here who
> shall do a great work in that land." Pointing to
> me, he said: "There is Anson, he shall go and
> shall assist in building up cities from one end of
> the country to the other, and you (rather extend-
> ing the idea to all those he had spoken of) shall
> perform as great a work as has been done by man,
> so that the nations of the earth shall be astonished,
> and many of them will be gathered in that land and
> assist in building cities and temples, and Israel
> shall be made to rejoice."

It is impossible to represent in words this
scene which is still vivid in my mind, of the grandeur of Joseph's appearance, his beautiful descriptions of this land, and his wonderful prophetic
utterances as they emanated from the glorious
inspiration that overshadowed him. There was a
force and power in his exclamations of which the
following is but a faint echo: "Oh, the beauty of
those snow-capped mountains! The cool refresh-
ing streams that are running down through those
mountain gorges!" Then gazing in another direction, as if there was a change of locality: "Oh, the
scenes that this people will pass through! The
dead that will lay between here and there." Then
turning in another direction as if the scene had
again changed: "Oh the apostasy that will take
place before my brethren reach that land! But,"

he continued, "the priesthood shall prevail over its enemies, triumph over the devil and be established upon the earth, never more to be thrown down!" He then charged us with great force and power, to be faithful to those things that had been and should be committed to our charge, with the promise of all the blessings that the Priesthood could bestow. "Remember these things and treasure them up. Amen."⁵⁰

With such clarity was the westward move of the Saints to the Rocky Mountains revealed to Joseph Smith that he later pointed out in some detail the course of their future travels. "One of the pioneers, George H. Goddard, . . . left on record the statement that he was present in the Masonic Hall in Nauvoo when Joseph Smith mapped out on the floor with a piece of chalk the Great Basin of western America, indicating the course they would follow across the continent."⁵¹ Hopkins C. Pendar also reported that "Joseph Smith, just before he was killed, made a sketch of the future home of the Saints in the Rocky Mountains and their route or road to that country as he had seen [it] in vision; a map or drawing of it." Levi W. Hancock either made this map as the Prophet pointed out the way or drew a copy of it, from which other copies were made. Brigham Young kept one copy, and "one was carried by the Mormon Battalion by which they knew where to find the church, or, Salt Lake Valley."⁵² Mosiah Hancock, son of Levi, threw further light on this matter when he gave the following account of the Prophet's visit to his father's home immediately before his departure for Carthage:

> ...the Prophet came to our home and stopped in our carpenter shop and stood by the turning

---

⁵⁰Edward W. Tullidge, *History of Northern Utah and Southern Idaho: Biographical Supplement,* pp. 271-272.

⁵¹E. Cecil McGavin, *Nauvoo the Beautiful* (Salt Lake City, 1946), p. 127.

⁵²"Diary of Oliver B. Huntington," *op. cit.,* p. 425.

lathe. I went and got my map for him. "Now,"
said he, "I will show you the travels of this people." He then showed our travels through Iowa,
and said, "Here you will make a place for the
winter; and here you will travel west until you
come to the valley of the Great Salt Lake! You
will build cities to the North and to the South,
and to the East and to the West; and you will
become a great and wealthy people in that land."[53]

In light of these reports, the testimony of William
Henry Kimball, son of Heber C. Kimball, is also interesting.
Kimball reported that he was present in the home of Stephen
Winchester, in Nauvoo, with twenty-five "staunch Saints,"
when Joseph Smith spoke of his coming martyrdom; and
"then and there he mapped [out] the life and acts of Brigham Young until [his] death." Said Kimball, "I can
assure you it never failed in one instance; I have witnessed
the fulfillment to all of the prophecy to a letter and act."[54]

Joseph Smith beheld the end from the beginning in his
vision of the kingdom of God and in his view of the great
panorama of events to be enacted in the last days. Of that
vision he said, "The work of the Lord in these last days is
one of vast magnitude and almost beyond the comprehension
of mortals."[55] But despite the magnitude of the program,
he claimed to understand it. "I have the whole plan of the
kingdom before me," he declared, "and no other person

---

[53]"The Life Story of Mosiah Lyman Hancock," typewritten copy in Brigham
Young University Library, pp. 27-29.
[54]Letter of William Henry Kimball to Emmeline B. Wells, written at Coalville
City, Summit Co., Utah, January 20, 1907. Original in Church Historian's Office,
Salt Lake City, Utah. The writer has corrected errors in spelling and punctuation. For a time during the early months of 1844 the Prophet considered settling
some of the Saints in Texas; and the possibility of moving the whole Church
to that area was also discussed. But in the closing weeks of his life he defi-
nitely settled upon the Great Salt Lake Basin. For a discussion of the Texas
proposal see Hyrum L. Andrus, *Joseph Smith and World Government* (Salt Lake
City, 1958), Chap. II.
[55]Cannon, *op. cit.,* p. 311.

has."[56]   That plan included a vision of events to occur in the latter days.

With the ushering in of the Dispensation of the Fulness of Times, when all things are eventually to be gathered together in Christ and placed under his law, the Lord declared that, unless men repent and embrace God's true plan of peace and union, an era of warfare and judgments would come upon the earth and terminate in universal chaos.[57]   In 1832, Joseph Smith recorded a revelation defining the broad course of international developments, beginning with the anticipated outbreak of civil war in America and leading from that point onward to the dissolution of the world's national-state system.[58]   Then, if not before, the Prophet held that the kingdom of God would spread throughout the earth, by conscientious men of all faiths embracing its political law.   Before that day, wars, conflicts, pestilences, and natural disturbances would follow one upon another "until the Ancient of Days comes, then judgment will be given to the Saints."[59]

Judgment under the kingdom of God will be fully given to the Saints only after Christ is crowned King of kings and Lord of lords, in the great council to be held at Adam-ondi-Ahman.   Here Adam, the Ancient of Days, will sit with all in ages past who have held the keys of priesthood authority on earth, under his direction.   Each will give an account of his stewardship; and having done so, all will then sustain Christ as the great Lawgiver of his kingdom, with the legal right to rule the earth.   The Saints will then be given dominion in righteousness; and from that

[56]*History of the Church*, V, p. 139.
[57]See Doctrine and Covenants 1:34-38; 5:19-20; 45:62-71; 49:9-10; 84:96-98; 112:23-26.
[58]*Ibid.*, 87.
[59]*History of the Church*, III, pp. 390-391.

time forward the millennial kingdom will extend its power unto victory.[60]

Joseph Smith gazed in vision upon the great events leading up to the full establishment of the kingdom of God and the dawn of millennial peace. In 1839, he made reference to that future era of universal chaos, when to live in peace men would have to flee to Zion and develop her powers abroad throughout the earth, and he said:

> The time is soon coming when no man will have any peace but in Zion and her stakes.
>
> I saw men hunting the lives of their own sons, and brothers murdering brother, women killing their own daughters, and daughters seeking the lives of their mothers. I saw armies arrayed against armies. I saw blood, desolation, fires.[61]

In 1823, Moroni taught Joseph Smith that the Zion of the latter-days would arise amid difficulties to sanctify the earth.[62] And a revelation, given March 7, 1831, described in some detail that future era, when the New Jerusalem is to be established as "a land of peace, a city of refuge, a place of safety for the saints of the Most High God." Explained the revelation:

> . . . and the glory of the Lord shall be there, and the terror of the Lord also shall be there, insomuch that the wicked will not come unto it, and it shall be called Zion.
>
> And it shall come to pass among the wicked, that every man that will not take his sword against his neighbor must needs flee unto Zion for safety.
>
> And there shall be gathered unto it out of

---

[60]See *ibid.*, pp. 385-392.
[61]*Ibid.*, pp. 390-391.
[62]*Messenger and Advocate*, October, 1835.

every nation under heaven; and it shall be the only
people that shall not be at war one with another.
And it shall be said among the wicked: Let us not
go up to battle against Zion, for the inhabitants
of Zion are terrible; wherefore we cannot stand.

And it shall come to pass that the righteous
shall be gathered out from among all nations, and
shall come to Zion, singing with songs of everlasting joy.[63]

Joseph Smith spoke repeatedy of these great events
of the latter-day, as he beheld them in vision. Oliver B.
Huntington reported that on one occasion the Prophet was
talking about the past history of the world,

... and when he came to the present times he
did not stop, but went on and related the principal
events that will transpire in the history of the
world down to the time when the angel will de-
clare that time shall be no longer.

Although I did not see the events with my
natural eyes, the vividness of their appearance to
my mind was next to reality.

He declared the succession of events with as
great clearness as one of us can repeat the events
of our past lives.[64]

Jedediah M. Grant, another intimate associate of the
Prophet, stated that three days before he started for
Carthage

The Prophet stood in his own house when
he told several of us of the night the visions of
heaven were opened to him, in which he saw the
American continent drenched in blood, and he saw
nation rising against nation. He also saw the

---

[63]Doctrine and Covenants 45:66-71.
[64]*Young Woman's Journal*, II, p. 467.

father shed the blood of the son, and the son shed
the blood of the father; the mother put to death
the daughter, and the daughter the mother; and
natural affection forsook the hearts of the wicked;
for he saw that the Spirit of God should be withdrawn from the inhabitants of the earth, in consequence of which there should be blood upon the
face of the whole earth, except among the people
of the Most High. The Prophet gazed upon the
scene his vision represented, until his heart sick-
ened and he besought the Lord to close it up
again.[65]

Joseph Smith was indeed a mighty seer. Through that
divine gift he gave the world other volumes of sacred
scriptures, to be new witnesses for Christ and for his gospel
in modern times. By vision he viewed the past and the
future of man's eternal existence and contemplated his
relationship to God and to Christ's eternal bar of judgment.
Joseph saw the latter-day Church and Kingdom, in every
detail of organization, and beheld their relationship to the
past and to the future. The great exodus of the Church
to the West, the establishment of the Saints as a mighty
people in the Rocky Mountains, and the future redemption
of Zion—all these events, with their attending developments, came within the scope of his vision. To him the past,
the present, and the future were one immediate moment;
and the end of that moment is not yet.

---

[65]*J. D.*, II, pp. 146-147.

VI.

Conclusions

Visions and revelations such as the Prophet experienced are centered in the operation of eternal law, and they bear the imprint of an infinite intelligence. This fact, along with the evidence of perfect consistency and inner union within the profound body of thought that came to him through his visions and revelations, argues strongly that Joseph Smith was in communion with God. Spiritual communion such as he received comes not to the natural man. Only those who put off the natural man, exercise true and living faith, and achieve a life of unfeigned righteousness can claim the right to such communion. A revelation explained that a "natural man [cannot] abide the presence of God, neither [he who is] after the carnal mind."[1]

Joseph Smith contended that "it is the first principle of the gospel to know for a certainty the character of God and to know that we may converse with Him as one man converses with another."[2] Power to do so is inseparably associated with the true gospel of Christ. To enjoy the full blessings of the gospel, one must follow the "established order of the kingdom of God" and come "unto the spirits of just men made perfect, and unto an innumerable company of angels, unto God the Father of all, and to Jesus Christ the Mediator of the new covenant."[3] But one does not attain unto such communion without great spiritual and character development. To quote the Prophet:

---

[1]Doctrine and Covenants 67:11-12.
[2]*Times and Seasons*, August, 1844. Statement made in April, 1844.
[3]*History of the Church*, VI, pp. 50-52.

We consider that God has created man with a mind capable of instruction, and a faculty which may be enlarged in proportion to the heed and diligence given to the light communicated from heaven to the intellect; and that the nearer man approaches perfection, the clearer are his views, and the greater his enjoyments, till he has overcome the evils of his life and lost every desire for sin; and like the ancients, arrives at that point of faith where he is wrapped in the power and glory of his maker and is caught up to dwell with Him. But we consider that this is a station to which no man ever arrived in a moment: he must have been instructed in the government and laws of that kingdom by proper degrees, until his mind is capable in some measure of comprehending the propriety, justice, equality, and consistency of the same.[4]

To receive such communion, ordinarily one must be justified, sanctified, and sealed by the powers of the gospel unto eternal life. In justification, the individual is freed from the demands of justice insofar as punishment for personal sins is concerned. Justification can be attained only by the grace of Jesus Christ, but to receive saving grace it is necessary to exercise true and living faith in Christ and in his atonement. That faith must be sufficient to motivate the individual to repent of all sin and to enter into covenant with Christ through baptism under his authority, for the remission of sins. These principles are termed the "preparatory gospel."[5] When one complies with them, the barriers between man and God are erased, and man is vindicated or acquitted of all sin. The individual is then in a position where the enlightening, purifying, and sealing powers of the gospel, as administered by the Holy Ghost through the higher ordinances thereof, can be extended unto him.

---

[4]*History of the Church,* II, p. 8.
[5]Doctrine and Covenants 84:26-27.

To be sanctified is to be purified and made holy "by the reception of the Holy Ghost."[6] These powers are administered only through the channels of the Melchizedek Priesthood. Worthy recipients of the priesthood and of its powers are "sanctified by the Spirit unto the renewing of their bodies,"[7] "which sanctification cometh because of their yielding their hearts to God."[8] Or, as a revelation to Joseph Smith explained, "Sanctification through the grace of our Lord and Savior Jesus Christ is just and true, to all those who love and serve God with all their mights, minds, and strength."[9] Says the Book of Mormon of those who, by the powers of the priesthood, were thus cleansed, "Now they, after being sanctified by the Holy Ghost, having their garments made white, being pure and spotless before God, could not look upon sin save it were with abhorrence; and there were many, exceeding great many, who were made pure and entered into the rest of the Lord their God."[10]

At a conference held October 25, 1831, "President Joseph Smith, Jun. said that the order of the Holy Priesthood was that they have power given them to seal up the Saints unto eternal life." But, he explained, "until the Saints had perfect love they were liable to fall. When they had a testimony that their names were sealed in the Lamb's book of life, they had perfect love, and then it was impossible for false Christ to deceive them."[11] Such love is made possible only when one receives and responds to the power of the Holy Ghost. Among other things, the Comforter fills worthy recipients of his power "with hope and perfect love."[12]

---

[6] 3 Nephi 27:19-21.
[7] Doctrine and Covenants 84:19-24, 33; Hebrews 7:11-12.
[8] Helaman 3:35.
[9] Doctrine and Covenants 20:31.
[10] Alma 13:7-16.
[11] Journal History, October 25, 1831. See also Far West Record, p. 16, under same date.
[12] Moroni 8:25-26.

124   JOSEPH SMITH, THE MAN AND THE SEER

To Joseph Smith, the gospel of Jesus Christ rests essentially upon a power principle—power to justify repentant man before the bar of God, power to sanctify and enlighten him, and power to develop him in love and in righteousness to where his calling and election is made sure; and then power to seal him up unto eternal life. Said the Prophet, "The more sure word of prophecy means a man's knowing that he is sealed up unto eternal life by revelation and the spirit of prophecy, through the power of the Holy Priesthood."[13] To a worthy colleague who had received the sealing powers and ordinances of the priesthood, Joseph said, "Nothing but the unpardonable sin can prevent you from inheriting eternal life for you are sealed up by the power of the Priesthood unto eternal life, having taken the step necessary for that purpose."[14]

---

[13]*History of the Church*, V, p. 392. The Prophet said on another occasion: Now for the secret and grand key. Though they might hear the voice of God and know that Jesus was the Son of God, this would be no evidence that their election and calling was made sure, that they had part with Christ, and were joint heirs with Him. They then would want that more sure word of prophecy, that they were sealed in the heavens and had the promise of eternal life in the kingdom of God. Then, having this promise sealed unto them, it was an anchor to the soul, sure and steadfast. Though the thunders might roll and lightnings flash, and earthquakes bellow, and war gather thick around, yet this hope and knowledge through our Lord and Savior Jesus Christ is the grand key that unlocks the glories and mysteries of the kingdom of heaven . . . and puts in our possession the glories of the celestial world. . . . Then I would exhort you to go on and continue to call upon God until you make your calling and election sure for yourselves, by obtaining this more sure word of prophecy, and wait patiently for the promise until you obtain it, &c.—*Ibid.*, pp. 388-389.

[14]*Ibid.*, p. 391. When a person develops to this point through the gospel, there are but two final alternatives before him. He might commit the unpardonable sin which would make of him a Son of Perdition. The Prophet explained: "According ot the Scripture, if men have received the good word of God, and tasted of the powers of the world to come, if they shall fall away, it is impossible to renew them again, seeing they have crucified the Son of God afresh, and put Him to an open shame; so there is a possibility of falling away; you could not be renewed again, *and the power of Elijah cannot seal against this sin, for this is a reserve made in the seals and power of the Priesthood.*"—*Ibid.*, VI, p. 253. (Italics by the writer.) But if the individual continues, after being sealed by the power of the priesthood, without committing the unpardonable sin, he will enter into his exaltation in the celestial kingdom. Should he, after being thus sealed, commit serious transgressions short of the unpardonable sin, the demands of eternal justice will be required at his hands, for the atonement of Christ will no longer cover his sins, but after making the necessary payment himself, he may then enter into his exaltation. The Prophet explained:

"The unpardonable sin [as it applies to individuals who are thus sealed] is to shed innocent blood, or be accessory thereto. All other sins will be visited

One who is spiritually mature enough to make his calling and election sure is entitled to receive what the Prophet referred to as the Second Comforter. Said he:

There are two Comforters spoken of. One is the Holy Ghost, the same as given on the day of Pentecost, and that all Saints receive after faith, repentance, and baptism. This first Comforter or Holy Ghost has no other effect than pure intelligence. . . .

The other Comforter spoken of is a subject of great interest, and perhaps understood by few of this generation. After a person has faith in Christ, repents of his sins, and receives the Holy Ghost, (by the laying on of hands), which is the first Comforter, then let him continue to humble himself before God, hungering and thirsting after righteousness, and living by every word of God, and *the Lord will soon say unto him, Son, thou shalt be exalted. When the Lord has thoroughly proved him, and finds that the man is determined to serve Him at all hazards, then the man will find his calling and election made sure, then it will be his privilege to receive the other Comforter, which the Lord hath promised the Saints,* as is recorded in the testimony of St. John, in the 14th chapter, from the 12th to the 27th verses. . . .

Now what is this other Comforter? It is no more nor less than the Lord Jesus Christ Himself; and this is the sum and substance of the whole matter; that when any man obtains this last Comforter, he will have the personage of Jesus Christ to attend him or appear unto him from time to time,

with judgment in the flesh, and the spirit being delivered to the buffetings of Satan until the day of the Lord Jesus."—*Ibid.*, V., pp. 391-392.

For another statement on this matter, see Doctrine and Covenants 132:26-27. In the writer's opinion, the sealing powers here referred to are only bestowed in conjunction with what the Latter-day Saints commonly term the "Second Anointing." A study of the historical context in which the Prophet recorded the above revelation and of statements he made on the subject during that period tends to support this conclusion.

and even He will manifest the Father unto him, and they will take up their abode with him, and the visions of the heavens will be opened unto him, and the Lord will teach him face to face, and he may have a perfect knowledge of the mysteries of the Kingdom of God; and this is the state and place the ancient Saints arrived at when they had such glorious visions—Isaiah, Ezekiel, John upon the Isle of Patmos, St. Paul in three heavens, and all the Saints who held communion with the general assembly and Church of the Firstborn.[15]

In emphasizing that spiritual maturity is necessary for one to receive the personal visitation of Christ, Joseph Smith was largely speaking out of the background of his own experience. He, like the ancient prophets, was one who had been foreordained to fill a mission of great importance in life; he was one of the great and noble spirits whom God chose to be his rulers.[16] And, like his predecessors in the prophetic line, the power of God was manifested in abundance through his ministrations.

To experience spiritual manifestations such as Joseph Smith and other prophets before him received, sanctified men must be quickened by the powers of God at the time of the given experience. A revelation explained, "No man has seen God at any time in the flesh, except quickened by the Spirit of God."[17] Moses, for example, was enveloped in the power and glory of God when he talked with that divine Personage, and later testified, "Now mine own eyes have beheld God; but not my natural, but my spiritual eyes, for my natural eyes could not have beheld; for I should have withered and died in his presence, *but his glory was upon me;* and I beheld his face, *for I was transfigured before*

---

[15]*History of the Church,* III, pp. 380-381. (Italics by the writer.)
[16]See Abraham 3:22-24.
[17]Doctrine and Covenants 67:11-12.

him."[18] While in the presence of God on another occasion, Moses absorbed the heavenly element in such degrees that "the skin of his face shone" with the glory of God, and he found it necessary to veil his face that he might speak to the Israelites.[19] Enoch, Abraham, and the brother of Jared had similar experiences.[20] The most widely known and accepted incident of this kind occurred to Jesus on what has since been called the Mount of Transfiguration. Of it the New Testament records:

> And after six days Jesus taketh with him Peter, and James and John, and leadeth them up into an high mountain apart by themselves; and he was transfigured before them. And his raiment became shining, exceeding white as snow; so as no fuller on earth can white them. And there appeared unto them Elias with Moses: and they were talking with Jesus.[21]

The visions and revelations given to Joseph Smith were also accompanied by an overshadowing power and glory visible to those present—not merely a change of facial expression resulting from a given mood or attitude of mind, but a thrilling, intelligent power both felt and seen by others. Orson Pratt testified that he saw the Prophet's "countenance light up as the inspiration of the Holy Ghost rested upon him dictating the great and most precious revelations now printed for our guide."[22] Jared Carter gave a corroborating testimony.[23] And Brigham Young said:

> Those who were acquainted with him knew when the Spirit of revelation was upon him for his

---

[18]Moses 1:2, 9-11, 31. (Italics by the writer.)
[19]Exodus 34:29-30; 2 Corinthians 3:7-13.
[20]See Moses 6:25-36; 7:3-4; Abraham 3:11-12; Ether 3.
[21]Mark 9:2-4; Luke 9:28-31.
[22]*J. D.*, VII, p. 176.
[23]*Journal History*, September 25, 1831

countenance wore an expression peculiar to him-self while under that influence. He preached by the Spirit of revelation, and taught in his council by it, and those who were acquainted with him could discover it at once, for at such times there was a peculiar clearness and transparency in his face.[24]

Emmeline B. Wells gave a similar testimony when she wrote of the Prophet:

He was beyond my comprehension. The power of God rested upon him to such a degree that on many occasions he seemed transfigured. His expression was mild and almost childlike in repose; and when addressing the people, who loved him it seemed to adoration, the glory of his countenance was beyond description. At other times the great power of his manner, more than of his voice (which was sublimely eloquent to me) seemed to shake the place on which we stood and penetrated the inmost soul of his hearers, and I am sure that then they would have laid down their lives to defend him.[25]

Several testimonies from independent sources corrobo-rate and elaborate upon the above statements. A young woman of about twenty years of age was working for the Whitmer family as a hired girl when Joseph and Oliver were completing the translation of the Book of Mormon at the Whitmer home. She later related that when they came down from the room in which they were working, "they looked so exceedingly white and strange that she inquired of Mrs. Whitmer the cause of their unusual appearance." Finally, Mrs. Whitmer "told her what the men were doing in the room above and that the power of God was so great

---

[24]*J. D.*, IX, p. 89.
[25]*Ibid.*, p. 556.

in the room that they could hardly endure it. At times angels were in the room in their glory which nearly consumed them."[26]

Philo Dibble reported that he "saw the glory and felt the power" that overshadowed Joseph Smith and Sidney Rigdon when the vision of the three degrees of glory was manifested, in February, 1832. Dibble explained further, "Joseph wore black clothes, but at this time seemed to be dressed in an element of glorious white."[27] While the Prophet was preaching in Mount Pleasant, Brant County, Ontario, Canada, in October, 1833, one who was present said that " his face became white and a shining glow seemed to beam from every feature."[28] And Mary Ann Winters spoke of a meeting in Nauvoo, at which Joseph Smith spoke to a group of Indians who had come to see him:

> I stood close by the Prophet while he was preaching to the Indians in the Grove by the Temple. The Holy Spirit lighted up his countenance till it glowed like a halo around him, and his words penetrated the hearts of all' who heard him and the Indians looked as solemn as Eternity.[29]

---

[26]Related to Oliver B. Huntington at a later date by the girl concerned in the experience. She joined the Church as a result of it and in her later years lived at Provo, Utah, where she told Huntington of the experience, and he in turn recorded it in his diary.—"Diary of Oliver B. Huntington," *op. cit.*, pp. 415-416. Oliver Cowdery wrote of the power associated with the translation of the Book of Mormon, stating: "These were days never to be forgotten—to sit under the sound of a voice dictated by the inspiration of heaven, awakened the utmost gratitude of this bosom!"—*Times and Seasons*, II, p. 201.

There is evidence that Joseph Smith was familiar with this transfiguring power early in his career. Reference is again made to the vision where he and Sidney Rigdon beheld the three degrees of glory. During the vision, Joseph "sat firmly and calmly" in the midst of "a magnificent glory," while Sidney "sat limp and pale" and "limber as a rag." In observing his companion, the Prophet afterward remarked: "Sidney is not used to it as I am."—*Juvenile Instructor*, XXVII, pp. 303-304. This experience occurred in February, 1832; and the Prophet's remark indicates that he had had considerable experience with that glorious power before that date.

[27]*Juvenile Instructor*, XXVII, pp. 303-304; *Faith Promoting Series: Eighth Book*, pp. 80-81.

[28]*Journal History*, October 29, 1833.

[29]*Young Woman's Journal*, XVI, p. 558.

Oliver B. Huntington was present and witnessed another incident of this kind. It occurred as the Prophet was acting as a prosecuting attorney in Nauvoo. Three of the brethren had been kidnapped by Missourians, taken to Missouri, and starved and whipped until they were hardly able to walk. Despite their physical condition they had managed to escape and return to Illinois where, some years later, one of them recognized a former assailant in disguise, walking the streets of Nauvoo. The kidnapper was brought before an alderman for trial, and Joseph acted as prosecuting attorney. During the trial the Prophet related the sufferings of the Saints at the hands of their enemies in Missouri, and then "went on to tell what Missouri should be called to endure in order to pay the penalty of wrongs inflicted and for the blood of the Saints they had shed." Huntington later wrote:

A portion of the words of the prophet I will quote verbatim: "She shall drink out of the same cup, the same bitter dregs we have drunk, poured out, out, out! and that by the hand of an enemy—a race meaner than themselves."

All the time he was delivering the word of the Lord his face shone as if there was a light within him and his face was translucent.

The time thus occupied was considerable, for he pronounced two other very remarkable prophecies.

When he had done prophesying he stopped speaking entirely, while he wiped a flood of perspiration from his face and gave vent to his pent-up breath with a long blow, kind of a half-whistle, and after a minute or two he remarked, "Well, where that meaner race is coming from God only knows. It is not the 'niggers,' for they don't know enough, and are gentlemen by the side of their masters. It is not the Indians, for they are the chosen people of God and a noble race of men, but as sure as God ever spoke by me that shall come to pass."

I have lived to see that prophecy literally fulfilled in the Rebellion [Civil War], when every family in that part of the state that the Saints used to occupy was killed or compelled to leave their homes by the Bushwackers or Guerillas under Quantrill—a generation of vipers raised up mostly after that prophecy was uttered.[30]

Another remarkable incident was reported by Mary Elizabeth Rollins Lightner, an early convert in the vicinity of Kirtland. Shortly after her conversion, Joseph Smith and others moved from New York to that vicinity in Ohio. Upon his arrival, the Prophet lived for a time in part of Newel K. Whitney's house. One evening shortly thereafter, Mary, with her mother, paid a visit to the Prophet's home to learn more of the Book of Mormon. Others had also gone that evening to see Joseph, and as they were gathered together he suggested that they hold a meeting. Said Sister Lightner:

> After prayer and singing, Joseph began talking. He began very solemnly and very earnestly. Suddenly, his countenance changed and he stood mute; he seemed almost transfixed. He was looking ahead and his face outshone the candle which was on a shelf just behind him. I thought I could almost see the cheek bones. He looked as though a searchlight was inside his face. I never saw anything like it on earth. I could not take my

---

[30]*Ibid.*, II, pp. 124-125. See also *Historical Record, op. cit.*, p. 536, for another report that Joseph Smith said of the enemies of the Saints in Missouri: "They shall drink a drink offering, the bitterest dreg, not from the 'Mormons,' but from a meaner source than themselves." William Quantrill, an American guerilla, first came to notoriety when he raided Lawrence, Kansas, killing 140 people and devastating the town. He continued his operations through western Missouri, where the Saints had previously been located, but upon attempting to extend his ravages into Kentucky, in 1864, he was killed. Many in Missouri were either killed or driven from their lands.

eyes away from him. I shall remember him as he
looked then as long as I live.

After a short time he looked at us very
solemnly, as if to pierce each heart, then said,
"Brothers and Sisters, do you know who has been
in your midst this night?"

One of the Smith family said, "An angel of
the Lord."

Joseph did not answer. Martin Harris was
sitting at the Prophet's feet on a box. He slid to
his knees, clasped his arms around the Prophet's
knees and said, "I know, it was our Lord and
Saviour, Jesus Christ."

Joseph put his hand on Martin's head and
answered, "Martin, God revealed that to you.
Brothers and Sisters, the Saviour has been in
your midst this night. I want you to remember it.
He cast a veil over your eyes for you could not
endure to look upon Him. You must be fed with
milk and not meat. I want you to remember this
as if it were the last thing that escaped my lips."[31]

The Prophet then knelt and prayed. "And such a
prayer, I never heard before or since," Sister Lightner
reported. "We all felt that he was talking to the Lord,
and the Spirit of the Lord rested down on the congregation."[32]

Shortly before his martyrdom, the Prophet spent much
time instructing the Twelve in the duties, powers, and
functions of the Church and the Kingdom of God. His
last speech to that body was another memorable occasion when the power and glory of God were manifested to
a remarkable degree. Wilford Woodruff recounted it
later:

---

[31]"Journal and Memoir of Mary Elizabeth Rollins Lightner," pp. 2-3; *Young
Woman's Journal*, XVI, pp. 556-557. The writer has combined the statements
made by Mrs. Lightner in these two sources in the above quote.
[32]*Idem.*

The last speech that Joseph Smith ever made
to the quorum of the Apostles was in a building
in Nauvoo, and it was such a speech as I never
heard from mortal man before or since. He was
clothed upon with the Spirit and power of God.
His face was clear as amber. The room was filled
as with consuming fire. He stood three hours
upon his feet. Said he: "You Apostles of the
Lamb of God have been chosen to carry out the
purposes of the Lord on the earth. Now I have
received, as the Prophet, Seer and Revelator,
standing at the head of this dispensation, every
key, every ordinance, every principle and every
priesthood that belongs to the last dispensation
and fulness of times. And I have sealed all these
things upon your heads."[33]

Wilford Woodruff repeatedly bore witness of this
event, declaring again on another occasion that the Prophet's
"face shone like amber."[34]   At a stake conference held in
Provo, Utah, April 20-21, 1895, he stated that he was
present "the last time that Joseph Smith the Prophet ever
met the quorum of the Twelve . . . and testified that Joseph
was transfigured before them."[35]   At a meeting of the First
Presidency, March 12, 1897, he said:

I bear my testimony that in the early spring
of 1844, in Nauvoo, the Prophet Joseph called
the Apostles together and he delivered unto them
the ordinances of the Church and Kingdom of
God, and all the keys and powers that God had
bestowed upon him, he sealed upon our heads,
and he told us we must round up our shoulders
and bear off this kingdom, or we would be
damned. I am the only man now living in the
flesh who heard that testimony from his mouth,

[33]*Conference Report,* April, 1898, p. 89.
[34]*Young Woman's Journal,* V (August, 1894), No. 11.
[35]"Diary of Oliver B. Huntington," *op. cit.,* p. 378.

and I know it was true by the power of God
manifest to him. At that meeting he stood on his
feet for about three hours and taught us the things
of the kingdom. His face was clear as amber,
and he was covered with a power that I had never
seen on any man in the flesh before.[36]

So much was Joseph Smith associated with spiritual
powers and to such an extent was he familiar with the intelligence that flowed therefrom that they became second
nature to him. He spoke and wrote continually in this
frame of reference. While studying the New Testament
in the Hebrew, Greek, Latin, and German languages, he
commented, "I have been reading the German, and find it
to be the most [nearly] correct translation, and to corre-
spond nearest to the revelations which God has given to
me for the last fourteen years."[37]   Again he said, "I have
got the oldest book in the world [the Bible]; but I [also]
have the oldest book in my heart, even the gift of the Holy
Ghost."[38] Finally, with emphasis:

> . . . I am learned, and know more than all the
> world put together. The Holy Ghost does, any-
> how, and He is within me, and comprehends more
> than all the world: and I will associate myself
> with Him.[39]

The Prophet taught that men should seek learning
"by study and also by faith."[40]   The two processes should
be co-ordinated, with the Holy Spirit acting as a guide
into all truth. Nevertheless, he emphasized, "the best way
to obtain truth and wisdom is not to ask it from books, but
to go to God in prayer, and obtain divine teachings."[41] He

---

[36]*Journal History*, under date.
[37]*History of the Church*, VI, p. 307.
[38]*Ibid.*, p. 308.
[39]*Idem.*
[40]Doctrine and Covenants 109:14.
[41]*History of the Church*, IV, p. 425.

said, "Could you gaze into heaven five minutes, you would know more than you would by reading all that ever was written on the subject."[42] Again, he commented, "Any person that has seen the heavens opened knows that there are three personages in the heavens who hold the keys of power, and one presides over all."[43]

These were not statements of hyperbole, but expressions that came from a sincere, earnest, and, at times, frustrated desire to awaken men to the reality of spiritual truth. Said the Prophet, "It is my meditation all the day, and more than my meat and drink, to know how I shall make the Saints of God comprehend the visions that roll like an overflowing surge before my mind."[44] Several times he exclaimed, "I would to God that I could unbosom my feelings in the house of my friends."[45] In a more jocular vein he said:

> There has been a great difficulty in getting anything into the heads of this generation. It has been like splitting hemlock knots with a corn-dodger for a wedge, and a pumpkin for a beetle. Even the Saints are slow to understand.
>
> I have tried for a number of years to get the minds of the Saints prepared to receive the things of God; but we frequently see some of them, after suffering all they have for the work of God, will fly to pieces like glass as soon as anything comes that is contrary to their traditions: they cannot stand the fire at all.[46]

While discussing this problem as it confronted Joseph Smith, John Taylor explained further:

---

[42]*Ibid.*, VI, p. 50.
[43]Franklin D. Richards and James A. Little, *A Compendium* (Salt Lake City, 1914), p. 261.
[44]*The Historical Record, op. cit.*, p. 512.
[45]*J. D.*, XXI, p. 317.
[46]*History of the Church*, VI, pp. 184-185.

No wonder that Joseph Smith should say that he felt himself shut up in a nutshell—there was no power of expansion; it was difficult for him to reveal and communicate the things of God, because there was no place to receive them. What he had to communicate was so much more comprehensive, enlightened and dignified than that which the people generally knew and comprehended, it was difficult for him to speak; he felt fettered and bound, so to speak, in every move he made.[47]

The forces of prejudice, tradition, and even unbelief hedged up the way and clogged the channel of communication between the Prophet and others. While in Kirtland, he said to Brigham Young, "Brother Brigham, if I was to reveal to this people what the Lord has revealed to me, there is not a man or woman would stay with me."[48] To others he declared that "what God commanded, the one half of the church would condemn."[49] Said Wilford Woodruff of the Prophet, "His mind was opened by the visions of the Almighty, and the Lord taught him many things by vision and revelation that were never taught publicly in his day; for the people could not bear the flood of intelligence which God poured into his mind."[50]

Despite the fact that the Saints loved and adored Joseph, few if any of them fully comprehended him. On several occasions he exclaimed, "Brethren, you do not know me, you do not know who I am."[51] George Q. Cannon later wrote:

> The Saints could not comprehend Joseph Smith; the Elders could not; the Apostles could not. They did so a little toward the close of his

---

[47]*J. D.,* X, p. 148.
[48]*Ibid.,* IX, p. 294.
[49]*Messenger and Advocate,* III (April, 1837), p. 487.
[50]*J. D.,* V, pp. 83-84.
[51]*Ibid.,* XXI, p. 317.

life; but his knowledge was so extensive and his comprehension so great that they could not rise to it.[52]

In the most famous of his recorded discourses, delivered shortly before his martyrdom, the Mormon Prophet made an appropriate comment on his interesting career when he declared:

> You don't know me; you never knew my heart. No man knows my history. I cannot tell it: I shall never undertake it. I don't blame any one for not believing my history. If I had not experienced what I have, I would not have believed it myself. . . . When I am called by the trump of the archangel and weighed in the balance, you will all know me then. I add no more. God bless you all.[53]

In concluding his essay on Joseph Smith, Josiah Quincy observed that while the Mormon leader had been "born in the lowest ranks of poverty, without booklearning and with the homeliest of all human names, he had made himself at the age of thirty-nine a power upon earth." Nor did the Prophet's martyrdom, in Quincy's estimation, mark the end of his influence. "Of the multitudinous family of Smith," he observed, "none had so won human hearts and shaped human lives as this Joseph."[54] Others also paid tribute to the greatness of Joseph Smith. A Boston editor spoke of him as a "genius—and a rare one."[55] And a writer in the *New York Sun* declared:

> This Joe Smith must be set down as an extraordinary character, a prophet-hero as Carlyle

[52]*Millennial Star*, LXI, p. 629.
[53]*History of the Church*, VI, p. 317.
[54]Quincy, *op. cit.*, p. 400.
[55]Reprinted in *Millennial Star*, III (August, 1842), pp. 65-66.

might call him. He is one of the greatest men of
the age and in the future will rank with those who,
in one way or another, have stamped their impression strongly on society.[56]

After considering the phenomenon of Mormonism and
its "master spirit," the Prophet, John Greenleaf Whittier
wrote:

> Once in the world's history we were to have a
> Yankee prophet, and we have had him in Joe
> Smith. For good or for evil, he has left his track
> on the great pathway of life; or, to use the words
> of Horne, "knocked out for himself a window in
> the wall of the nineteenth century," whence his
> rude, bold, good humored face will peer out upon
> the generations to come.[57]

Those who were personally acquainted with Joseph
Smith appreciated even better the greatness of the man
and the seer. Edward Stevenson, who "looked upon him
as upon no other man," said that he "began to believe that
the Prophet possessed an infinity of knowledge."[58] George
Q. Cannon, one of the Church's great minds, concurred
when he declared, "There was no end scarcely, in many
respects, to the knowledge that he received."[59] Orson Pratt
proclaimed that Joseph Smith was "one of the greatest men
who ever lived in this probation, one of the greatest Prophets, with the exception of our Lord and Savior Jesus Christ,
ever sent to our earth."[60] John Taylor wrote, and the
Saints have accepted it as canonized truth, that "Joseph
Smith, the Prophet and Seer of the Lord, has done more,

---

[56]Cited in *Stories about Joseph Smith the Prophet*, pp. 13-14.
[57]John Greenleaf Whittier, *Howitt's* Journal, as quoted in *Millennial Star*, X
(October 1, 1848), pp. 302-303.
[58]Joseph Grant Stevenson, "The Life of Edward Stevenson," unpublished
Master's Thesis, Brigham Young University, p. 85.
[59]*J. D.*, XXIII, p. 362.
[60]*Ibid.*, XVI, p. 327.

save Jesus only, for the salvation of men in this world, than any other man that ever lived in it."[61]

Joseph the Prophet and the Seer was chosen and foreordained of God to usher in the last and greatest dispensation of gospel truth and power ever revealed to man on earth. The work he was instrumental in establishing is here to purify the world of unrighteousness, to establish the millennial society of peace and prosperity throughout the earth, and to prepare all things for the reign of Christ. To initiate this titanic task and to lay the foundation upon which the perfected superstructure will one day rest, God chose a select seer, with spiritual, mental, and moral powers suited to the work at hand, and with personality and physical strength to bear the burden of that great responsibility. Said the editor of the *Millennial Star,* shortly after the Prophet's martyrdom:

The personal frame of Mr. Smith was fitted by nature for the greatest measure of endurance. His gigantic mind disposed of cares and troubles of a domestic, political, and religious character, with extraordinary tact; and scarcely could the fury of the storm have begun to abate, before the sunbeams of cheerfulness irradiated his countenance, and the versatile character of his mind allowed him rest and recreation, while others would have sunk despondingly under accumulated troubles. Conscious of possessing a knowledge of the most profound principles of truth, virtue, and happiness, that were ever revealed to man, he dealt out unsparing giant blows against the Goliath of error, and smiled alike at the formidable front of his antagonist, and the inevitable discomfiture that ensued. He contemplated, without shadow of doubt, the complete and triumphant success of that system of truth that God had re-

[61]Doctrine and Covenants 135:2.

vealed through him, for the temporal, spiritual,
and eternal safety of man; and although his days
were cut short by the cruel hands of assassins,
yet he lived to accomplish the work to which he
was sent.   This work he finished—the foundation
of the millennial reign was fully laid by him—
the superstructure is to go up to its full completion
with shoutings of grace—grace unto it.[62]

The words of Wilford Woodruff are fitting as a conclusion to this brief analysis of Joseph Smith.   After
listening to the Prophet address the Saints in the power and
demonstration of the Spirit, he recorded in his *Journal*:

There is not so great a man as Joseph standing in this generation.   The gentiles look upon him
and he is like a bed of gold concealed from human
view.   They know not his principles, his spirit,
his wisdom, his virtues, his philanthropy, nor his
calling. His mind, like Enoch's expands as eternity, and only God can comprehend his soul.[63]

---

[62]*Millennial Star*, IX (April 1, 1847), p. 104.
[63]*Journal History*, April 9, 1837.

Index